ADVANCE PRAISE

"During his more than 20 years in Japan, Paul Dupuis discovered the secrets which are at the heart of the Japanese leader. *The E5 Movement* is a unique, insightful blend of Western and Eastern beliefs painting a crystal clear picture of the power of the leader to do well, and do good."

KEN HONDA, Bestselling author, *Happy Money*, and renowned coach

"*The E5 Movement* is a fresh approach to leadership, written by someone who has first-hand experience leading transformation across borders. Full of real stories from the front line and strongly rooted in purpose, it's an insightful read for all leaders."

BEN RENSHAW, Author, *Purpose*

Published by
LID Publishing Limited
The Record Hall, Studio 304,
16-16a Baldwins Gardens,
London EC1N 7RJ, UK

info@lidpublishing.com
www.lidpublishing.com

A member of:

businesspublishersroundtable.com

Printed by Gutenberg Press, Malta
ISBN: 978-1-912555-78-9

Cover and page design: Matthew Renaudin

THE E5 MOVEMENT

LEADERSHIP THROUGH
THE RULE OF FIVE

PAUL DUPUIS

MADRID | MEXICO CITY | LONDON
NEW YORK | BUENOS AIRES
BOGOTA | SHANGHAI | NEW DELHI

CONTENTS

ACKNOWLEDGMENTS

Writing this book has been full of twists and turns, with plenty of discoveries along the way – a lot like my own leadership journey!

I'm grateful to the many leaders who have inspired me over the years, not only through their words but also through their actions. They include my high school teachers in Windsor, Ontario, especially Ron Barr and Patricia 'Ma' Creede who helped me navigate the teenage years and set me on a path to make an impact. My hockey and baseball coaches, especially Coach Ouellette, my high school football coach who taught me the importance of focus, composure and hard work. My foremen in the pressure-cooker on the assembly line at Chrysler. My leaders in business, especially Nick Johnston who taught me some of the key secrets of building high performing teams – define the culture, get the right people on the bus and strive to be better every day.

To the leaders who have mentored me over the years, and to the leaders who I've had the great pleasure to guide and advise on their own mission to lead with impact. The E5 was born from my own experiences and from observing others, but what made it 'real' was witnessing it in practice with my own teams. There's no greater joy as a leader than to see your team members grow, learn, achieve and then go on to help others to do the same. Cameron, Yusuke, Shun, Thomas, Vishy, Anjali and Yeshab, and many more … may you continue to shine and raise your own armies of game-changing leaders. This virtuous cycle makes it all worth the effort.

To my friends and colleagues who have nudged, advised and encouraged me along the way as I wrote this book; Mike Carroll, Vinay Kumar, Manjulakshmi Panicker, Gil Schwank, Janaki Rajagopalan, Bindu Mani, Anurag Batra, Jos Schut, Frank Ribuot and Sachin Chowdhery. And special thanks to Ken Honda, an incredible author and influencer who has become my mentor on this amazing journey from taking my thoughts about leadership and putting the pen to paper. His simple but profound words, "Paul, it's time to share your unique ideas with the world. Write your book," led to what would eventually become *The E5 Movement*.

And finally, to my family for their never-ending support and patience. My mother and father who taught me the true meaning of commitment, and gave me my most powerful mantra which carries me through the rough times: "*this too shall pass.*" My brothers, Chris and Mark, both exceptional leaders in their community. My sons Kengo and Seigo, global citizens, remarkable young men and future leaders in their own right, always feeding my fire with positivity and new ideas. And to my wife, Mika, my rock and my confidante. For her incredible patience on the many late nights as I wrestled with this book, to those early mornings, writing away on our balcony as the sun came up. The bottomless cups of coffee (and the extra-dark chocolate) which she prepared kept me fuelled up and focused on my mission to start a leadership movement. Get the kettle ready, there's more to come!

INTRODUCTION

The world is full of competent managers. These are the people who follow processes and meet deadlines. They run a tight ship and deliver on expectations. They focus on playing the game well. But they don't *change the game.*

Outstanding leaders, on the other hand, operate on a different level. They're not satisfied with 'good.' They're constantly searching for empty spaces, the opportunities to be a pioneer, to bring bold and ambitious ideas to life, and to create movements. These leaders not only play the game well, they are on a relentless mission to *change* the game and, ultimately, to *create a new game.*

Whether you lead a large global organization, a small business or a nongovernmental organization (NGO), or you are an established CEO, the veteran captain of your team or a first-time leader, we all have a desire to be part of something special.

In this book, we will look at game-changing leaders from the worlds of business, sports, politics and religion. We'll learn how they took a bold vision and brought it to life, and how they changed the world in their own way.

Over the years, I've closely observed leaders around me while I practised leadership along the way. In the process, I discovered some patterns among great leaders, which helped me create my own version of leadership. It's a formula of sorts, but certainly not a cookie-cutter prescription. I call it the 'E5', the most crucial elements and triggers of leadership, which are: envision, express, excite, enable and execute. Consider the E5 to be a framework, or better yet, a customizable recipe for game-changing leadership.

As a leader, you carry an important responsibility: to craft a vision that touches the hearts and minds of your team. To bring this vision into the world. To inspire to action. To create a movement. To enable others with the necessary tools, skills and support to move the wheels. And then, to make the ultimate move as a game-changing leader – to bring your vision to life. Each of us has a unique and powerful signature. This book will help you create your own '-ism' of leadership.

This book is not a theoretical study – it's about action. While the E5 is a formula, it's not rigid, and it's certainly not the one and only model. I hope that this book will help you learn from the exceptional leaders among us. And that you'll identify your strengths, leverage your experiences, take a bold dream and bring it to life. Ultimately, I hope the E5 will help you be the game changer.

So, in the spirit of keeping it simple, let's begin.

CHAPTER 1

MY ACCIDENTAL
ENCOUNTER
WITH LEADERSHIP

It was 5 September 1990. I remember the moment clearly.

I was 22 years old and about to board my flight at Detroit Metro airport, bound for Osaka, Japan. I felt all the emotions of a big kid about to experience a series of 'first times.' I was leaving home for the first time. I was on an airplane for the first time. I was traveling to a very foreign land, where I knew absolutely no one and had virtually no knowledge of its culture and language.

That sense of adventure, of reckless abandon, would pop up time and time again in the years that followed. What I lacked in preparedness, though, I made up for with an intense curiosity and desire to explore my world. Little did I know that what was intended to be a six-month adventure would turn into a lifetime voyage, an odyssey in which leadership would play an increasingly central role.

My fascination with Asia and the martial arts was the starting point of my accidental journey to leadership. I had worked for four years as a welder at the Chrysler minivan assembly plant in Windsor. This helped me pay for university, while also teaching me some valuable lessons about leadership. In fact, I saved every penny I could during university, foregoing spring break and skiing trips with buddies, using duct tape to repair my old ice hockey equipment and driving an old four-cylinder car on its last legs back and forth to school and to the factory. Over the years, my bank account slowly grew. I named it the 'Adventure Fund,' set aside specifically for this journey to Asia.

I saved up my coins and managed to gather enough to buy a ticket to Beijing. China was my first choice, the roots of the martial arts. My plan was to go directly to the Shaolin Temple, made famous in the old TV series *Kung Fu*. Just like David Carradine, I planned to shave my head, knock on the big wooden temple gate, bow deeply, be granted access as a student and, hopefully, one day earn the nickname 'grasshopper.' In hindsight, it was good to be young and fearless.

But, as I learned the hard way, things don't always go as planned. In 1989, shortly before I was scheduled to depart for China, a student protest in Beijing escalated to the point where it became a riot. I quickly learned a lesson in leadership and the power of the 'veto' when my Mom and Dad suggested (aka commanded): "Take your ticket back to the travel agent, you're not going to China." My ticket was refunded and deposited back into the 'Adventure Fund' account, but I was crushed.

Growing up in the 1970s and 1980s, when you were curious and needed information and knowledge, you had a couple of choices. One was to go to the bookshelf in the bedroom, pull out a volume from the family's *Encyclopedia Britannica* collection and flip through the pages until you found your topic. Or you could go to the local library. Since I had already absorbed every page in the encyclopaedia about China, I chose the second option and made a beeline to the Windsor Public Library. I made my way to the Asia section on the fourth floor and laid my hands on an edition of *The Lonely Planet*.

I pulled the book about Japan off the shelf, sat down and opened the door to a new world of discovery. I was absolutely fascinated. And so Japan it was, as I embarked on an adventure to discover myself and my world.

This adventure to Japan established a pattern of stepping out of my comfort zone on a regular cadence. It happened in 1990, shortly after I arrived in Japan. I had secured a job at a small private English-language school. Two weeks later, the entire staff of 12 teachers abruptly left the school due to a conflict with the owner. This new guy – me, just off the plane from Canada – was asked to be the school manager. It happened again in 1995 when I started a new life in a new city, Vancouver, Canada. Shortly after starting as a bellman and concierge at a five-star hotel, I was offered a management path. It repeated in 2011, when I relocated to a brand-new place, Singapore, to be Head of Asia Pacific. And again in 2013, when I moved to Tokyo as Managing Director of a large multinational company in the staffing and outsourcing industry. With nearly 100 offices, employees scattered across the country and a deep local culture, the challenge was immense. In 2017, I boarded a plane to live yet another voyage of discovery in India. And the adventure continues …

What's interesting is that most of these leadership opportunities were 'accidental.' I say accidental because they weren't my intended path, nor my goal. As I came to learn, many leaders end up in a role leading people not by design, but by accident. And these accidents provide us with moments of truth, opportunities to discover and grow. What follows next sets the difference between the competent manager and the game-changing leader.

After spending time with and observing leaders over the years, a few things have become increasingly clear. Competent managers 'maintain.' They protect and defend. And they work hard to maintain the status quo. Game-changing leaders, on the other hand, seek out opportunities to operate on the edge of their comfort zones, and they usually thrive well outside of it.

In his book *Alive at Work*, Dan Cable calls this curiosity and pursuit of knowledge and new experiences the "seeking system."[1] As human beings, we all possess a unique ability to be curious, and to make a conscious decision to lean into it. The leader who understands this and focuses on activating this curiosity in the teams they lead, has the potential to create a movement.

Leadership is a sword that needs to be constantly sharpened. The leader learns, then practises, reflects and gains valuable lessons. It's a virtuous cycle, which needs constant effort to gain momentum. Leadership is a muscle that needs to be exercised in order to grow stronger. Game-changing leaders, then, enjoy studying and practising leadership – this is how they sharpen their swords. And, leadership is about doing. As Yoda wisely said, *"No! Try not! Do or do not. There is no try."* Just like Michael Jordan, when he famously said, *"You miss more shots than you make."*

The game-changing leader embraces opportunity, cherishes and takes advantage of the moment to take that shot. More often than not, especially in the early days as a new leader, we goof up. This is part of the journey. Our failures become our successes when we learn from them and make a clear effort to improve as a result. A guiding mantra that serves all leaders well is: "When in doubt, go for it!" More simply put, you don't know until you go.

So *just go*.

CHAPTER 2

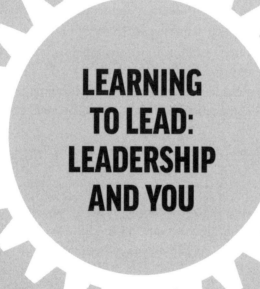

LEARNING TO LEAD: LEADERSHIP AND YOU

When I think about my journey as a leader, I have flashbacks to the neighbourhood park in my hometown in Canada. As a kid, during the summer holidays, I used to play baseball with my buddies on the baseball diamond. There was no captain; we were just a bunch of kids gathering at the park. Someone would inevitably step up and say, "OK guys, let's make teams." We would pick the players, decide positions, agree on the basic rules and throw the first pitch. This was repeated on the neighbourhood basketball court and on our backyard ice rink, where I chased my first passion, ice hockey. Kids coming together in a newly formed team, with a common purpose. And when disagreements arose (and they often did!), we decided whether the runner was safe or out, the lay-up was traveling or not, and whether the defensemen tripped the opponent on the breakaway.

No referees, no parents, no executive authority. Simply leaders *stepping up*.

I recall one time when I was eight or nine years old – we were playing street hockey with some older kids. One of our players was checked and knocked down on the concrete, knees cut up and bleeding. We had no referee to draw the line between right and wrong. I remember standing up to the big kids and saying, "Hey, wait a minute. You can't do that!" A debate ensued, pushing and shoving followed. I persisted, held firm and eventually we agreed that the player should sit out for two minutes. Justice was done. And the game continued.

My leadership journey clearly has its roots on those playgrounds, basketball courts and ice rinks. Looking back, I was usually one of those to *step up* – to organize, instigate, mediate or collaborate. I was rarely the best player on the team, though. But somehow, I was often selected to be the captain of my team. As I reflected on this over the years, it became clear that I had the ability to bring teams together, set goals, settle disputes, inspire my teammates to dig in and help others bring out their best. It's a quality that has come to serve me well in the various leadership challenges I've faced over the years. When it comes to game-changing leadership, this is a critical trait: the ability to assemble a diverse team of players, to help them perform at a higher level, to exceed expectations and to achieve a bold and ambitious goal.

Many leaders who I meet share similar stories of their own journey of taking leadership roles, sometimes voluntarily and sometimes selected by others. Where does this come from? It's a question that many leaders ask themselves, and a tough one to answer. When we're born, leadership is not part of the package. Contrary to what many leadership gurus will profess, leadership is not innate. It is a learned trait. We learn about leadership by watching our mothers and fathers, brothers and sisters, teachers, religious leaders, politicians, coaches and our peers. And as we move into the world of work, we have our first experience of formal leadership: our manager.

With firm building blocks, my notion of leadership has evolved over time. In my earlier years, I believed leadership was simply about getting things done and being a strong player. I thought it was about power, until my first real encounter with leadership in my senior year of high school, when I was elected Student

Council President. I now had the title and the authority that it brought, and assumed I would be able to "make people do what I wanted them to do." Needless to say, I learned a valuable lesson about the true meaning of leadership that year. Leadership, and the followership it breeds, does not come automatically. It must be earned.

Sounds familiar? Many leaders I meet with today face the same challenges in their own organizations. On the other hand, there is a wonderful sense of exhilaration in working together with teams to achieve a common goal. This feeling of fulfilment is a high, and for many leaders it's the main thing that gets them out of bed every morning.

Here's the good news. Any one of us can be a leader – and even better – a game-changing leader. Leadership is learned. It's built through experience. It's born in opportunities to influence others, whether on the playground, in your home or in the boardroom. And the best part is that leadership doesn't require a title.

Becoming an exceptional leader takes effort, focus, commitment, a strong sense of self-awareness and plenty of humility. Leadership is defined by behaviour. Exceptional leadership then, requires exceptional behaviour.

The leaders I've met over the years come from diverse backgrounds: men and women, charismatic and introverted, young and mature. In fact, when it comes to the profile of the transformative leader, there is no pattern. But it's interesting to observe that the exceptional leaders around us display some very similar behaviours.

They walk the talk and don't wear their title on their sleeve. Deep down, the best leaders are simply one of the crew. These leaders show conviction and courage in making decisions. They listen, gather facts and are not afraid to be the only one in the room who believes the decision is the right one. They think about the greater good, the positive impact of making their vision a reality.

There are some universal truths when it comes to exceptional leadership. It's evident in virtually all of the companies that experienced a transformation in extremely challenging situations. It's also apparent in the world of sports. There are many examples of teams that surprised the world by winning – these were the underdogs, the teams that weren't supposed to win. But they did. They won because of a compelling vision, driven by leaders committed to bringing their vision to life.

In Jim Collins' ground-breaking book *Good to Great*,[2] he takes a close look at the leaders of 11 companies that went from good to great. That is, the companies that transformed themselves as leaders in their industry, delivering significant returns to shareholders, and outperforming their competitors through economic cycles. These leaders built sustainable organizations that were future-proofed. He called them Level 5 Leaders. As he looked at the behaviours of these exceptional leaders, he discovered something very revealing. The leaders with impact had common traits, beginning with humility. These leaders were not seeking personal glory but, instead, their mission was focused on helping the organization thrive. Next, they shared the spotlight when they achieved success. And, in turn, when things went wrong, they were the first to accept responsibility.

One discovery was particularly revealing. These leaders were, more often than not, quite shy. They lacked the gregarious energy on stage that you would expect from a strong leader. But what they lacked in charisma, they made up for in their fearlessness in making tough decisions. And they were fierce in their conviction to bring their vision to life.

Somewhere along my own leadership journey, I discovered that leadership is not about one particular skill or behaviour. For years, I observed exceptional leaders around me and started to see something that eventually led me to write this book. Leaders come in all shapes and sizes, from the introverted, brilliant visionary to the larger-than-life charismatic leader. On the surface, they may appear to be worlds apart. But when we lift the layers and look at how they lead, a very interesting pattern emerges. The leaders who make an impact are fiercely committed to bringing their vision to life, and applying their strengths to make it happen.

Every machine that involves movement has interdependent parts, each of which plays a key role in making the machine work. Take the mechanical watch, for example. Movement is created through a series of gears, which drive a weighted wheel, which, in turn, oscillates back and forth at a constant rate. Next, a device called an escapement releases the watch's wheels to move forward – and with each swing of the balance wheel, the hands of the watch move ahead. All of this happens millions of times over the course of the life of a watch. But the only question we ask when we look at our watch is, "What time is it?"

I started to think about how these wheels, or cogs as they are sometimes called, could be connected to what we do every day as leaders. And I realized that much like the intricate movements of the components inside the watch, leadership is about creating movement. It's about influence. And influence doesn't happen by being a one-dimensional visionary or an inspirational leader. It's a combination of many elements, intricate and interdependent.

Game-changing leadership is universal, borderless, and immune to time and place. It's a series of wheels that work together to form a much larger wheel – the E5.

LEADERSHIP **AND YOU**

As a new leader, or as someone taking up a challenging next-level leadership role, you may ask yourself, "Can I do this?" It's a fair question. You want the opportunity, someone believes you have the right stuff, and the affirmation makes you feel proud.

But deep down inside, you wonder if you have the *right stuff* to do it. The new leadership role is outside of your comfort zone. It may be a team comprised of new people, or your peers, some who don't know you or at least haven't experienced you as their leader. Your new team hasn't been part of your journey. In their minds, you're just the 'new manager.' You need to earn your credibility as their leader.

The leadership journey is full of moments of truth. Taking on a new role and leading in a foreign environment is a challenge. Early on, after taking on the role, you may even ask yourself,

"What have I done?" The good news is that this is a completely normal and healthy response. When we step outside of our comfort zone and into a pressure cooker where there are high expectations with people relying on us to show them the way, there is a natural 'flight-or-fight' response that kicks in. The mix of emotions as a new leader is powerful. And this is the moment where game-changing leaders shine.

Perhaps the most extreme example of stepping outside the comfort zone as a leader is the senior leader who has built a long and successful career in a particular industry, earning accolades and credibility along the way. An expert in the domain with a track record of delivering results. And then, this leader accepts a senior position in a completely new arena. Moving from a comfortable place where the leader had virtually no blind spots to a world where there are *only* blind spots. Sounds like a bad decision? But the data tells us something different ...

Recently, I participated in an intensive programme on trans-formative leadership at the London Business School. We looked at leaders who came into CXO roles, moving from a similar role in a company in the same industry. That is, leaders with direct experience at the same level and industry, sort of like moving from Coke to Pepsi or from GM to Ford. We then compared the results that these leaders generated based on total shareholder return, employee engagement and sustainability versus leaders who were industry outsiders, with no prior experience in the role.

It's interesting to note that a CEO Success Study by PWC[3] found that industries that face an increasing level of disruption hire a higher proportion of outsiders. This is especially true in the telecom, energy and healthcare industries. It would have been unthinkable to hire senior leaders for organizations with little or no experience in the specific industry. However, this is exactly what's happening in recent years. These external hires bring fresh perspective and, because they're not insiders, they're allowed and encouraged to be curious, which, in turn, often results in new discoveries and opportunities. The simple and powerful question typically asked by these new leaders, "Why do we do it like that?" is often the trigger for change. As my former boss used to advise me, "Put your shovel in the ground again until you find the answer to the why."

At face value, hiring a CEO or a senior leader in a critical role from outside the industry seems to defy logic. Many in the organization will openly question the move by the board until the new leader starts to make decisions that bring change for the better. As a result, many organizations have started to realize that bringing in fresh perspective equates to diversity. And we all know now that diverse teams are stronger teams.

In my role as CEO of a large, complex services organization, I have the opportunity to meet leaders of all levels and from various walks of life. Many ask for my advice as they navigate their careers. Ask yourself the same question I ask them: "How does what you've done so far connect with what you aspire to do next in your leadership journey?" Most leaders are pretty good at sharing their story, talking about their university days, and the organizations they were a part of. But some others share thoughts on their discoveries and how they've grown along the way.

Many of us tend to default to our resumé and end up giving mini-advertorials about our organizations rather than focus on the path travelled and the learning along the way. My advice is to look at your resumé through new lenses, like a scavenger hunt, collecting tools and building new muscles along the way. And when the discussion turns to "what's next?" my recommendation is simple. If you're really hungry to grow as a leader, take risks, leave your comfort zone, and the further, the better! Game-changing leaders seek out moments of stress. They thrive under pressure. You can learn to constantly hone your skills and keep your sword sharp in a pressure cooker situation. You can go through the discomfort of starting new, and through all of this you'll learn to find your way. Be the leader who doesn't say, *"I know."* Instead, be the leader who says, *"I want to know."*

Some of the best advice I ever received was from a leader years ago, when I was about to start a new challenge in a new environment. He said, "Just be you."

You've come this far because of *you*, because of everything *you* bring to the table. This makes *you* unique and special as a leader and, most importantly, the parts that make *you* human. Your values, your behaviour in good times and bad, and even your sense of humour all come together to form your personal brand of leadership. The E5 is about creating your own version of leadership and a formula to ignite it.

Game-changing leaders are inherently restless. They're always looking for that new opportunity to discover something, to learn and to grow. It's this wanderlust spirit that has taken me all over the world – but I still remember and cherish my roots in Canada. The experiences I had growing up in Windsor, Ontario, made me who I am. The sense of community, volunteerism and the strong work ethic that is at the core of a blue-collar town helped form me as a leader. We take our values with us wherever we go. And these values, which are at our core, are with us not only from Monday to Friday; they become part of who we are. The authentic leader isn't scared of being human. In fact, it's this element that helps make them so effective.

Leadership is the core of who you are. Leadership is more than a responsibility – it's a vocation. And to be an exceptional leader, you should take this responsibility seriously, honouring your role through your words and actions. If all of that seems heavy, it's a good sign – being entrusted to be a leader of people is not to be taken lightly.

The E5 is a simple set of guidelines based on years of observations, discussions (sometimes hot debates!) and personal practice. In the process of reading about each E, you may find that something makes sense to you. On the other hand, you may find some elements to be confusing. In either case, if your interest is sparked and you want to learn more, we've included some tips and tricks and golden nuggets in each chapter for you to use in your own leadership journey. And, in the spirit of 'the answers are in the room,' we've created a community of fellow leaders who are on a mission to join the game-changing movement. These will help guide you as we learn from other leaders who have walked ahead of us.

This book is not a 'one-size-fits-all' manual to make you a cookie-cutter leader. The leader who fits in the box doesn't change the world, they simply maintain the status quo. Not necessarily a bad thing but, let's face it, if you have the will and the opportunity to change the world, I say, go for it!

We can all gain by taking the time to learn about leadership. Hopefully, through these pages of conversations, you can find some golden nuggets, things that you can use in your own role as a leader. And maybe you won't find the right nugget the first time around. I encourage you to revisit each chapter from time to time as you move along your own leadership journey. As I've found that whenever I reach for my favourite books on the shelf and reread a chapter, a new discovery, a golden nugget, inevitably emerges.

The fact that you're reading this book means you're probably on a search for that secret sauce, something to turbocharge your own personal mission. I hope that the E5 will be one book on your shelf that's opened and reopened, from time to time, as you move forward on your own quest to change the game.

Here we go …

CHAPTER 3

ENVISION

Your bold vision needs to be rooted in
the 'why,' the greater purpose.

have often thought about Martin Luther King, Jr's words ("I have a dream ...") in the context of game-changing leadership. Reverend King painted a vivid picture of what his new world looked like. A world where people would be equal. A nation where everyone would be free to speak their minds, be happy, and able to live feeling safe and at peace.

In his historic speech, he managed to 'push the buttons' of not only African Americans, but all Americans. It no longer became an issue of blacks and whites, nor an issue of division – it was about unity as a nation undivided. And by appealing to this common shared value of what it means to be an American.

Right there, right then, he had transformed his dream into a universal vision. You could say that Martin Luther King, Jr, through this one single speech, ignited the fire that led to immense change for the better. This is what impactful leaders have in common. They begin with a compelling vision – a vision that moves the heart and mind to action. Then they take action ... and they change the world.

What does it take to bring a compelling vision to life, to take it from a passing thought, from a bold dream to reality? Is there a magic step-by-step formula to actually make it happen? The power to envision and ignite the passion and the magic of the people you lead – at the core, this is the stuff that exceptional leadership is made of. The vision becomes the North Star, a guiding light as you create strategy with your team. It's the first crucial step toward making an impact as a leader.

Let's go back to Reverend King's vision and take a closer look. It was simple, yet bold. It was provocative and, yes, even scary. And it had one crucial piece that is absolutely key for impact. He addressed the 'why', the greater purpose.

Some would say that vision, mission and values are separate animals and the lines between each shouldn't be blurred. Let's agree that the vision is an aspirational view of the future, the mission explains why the organization exists and the values talk about what the organization stands for. All of this serves to guide the strategy to achieve the goals of the organization. So, when you boldly put your stake in the ground, and commit to a vision – whether it's been conceived by you or co-created from the bottom up – it inevitably leads to the 'why.' You simply can't separate the 'what' from the 'why.' They are intertwined. And when you weave them together, the potential to create an unstoppable movement is immense.

Due to the nature of my role, I meet daily with leaders from all walks of life. From the top leaders (CEOs, COOs, Heads of Sales, CHROs) to the front-line first-time leaders and new managers, there is a common question that comes out in our discussions: "How can I lead my team to achieve an ambitious goal, to get them on board and achieve new heights along the way?" The simple answer is clear. It begins with the captain of the ship.

I've sat with many CEOs over the years to discuss their strategy to take their organization to the next stage. Most leaders are proud to share their grand vision, and they should be. For this is at the core of what effective leaders do – craft a vision

"WHEN THE WHY IS CLEAR, THE HOW IS EASY."

JIM ROHN

and share it with others. Unfortunately, for many, the grand vision becomes *too grand*, morphing uncontrollably into a detailed, multi-slide dissertation encompassing not only the vision, but diving deep into the how, and the metrics associated with the expected outcomes. Of course, the leader believes the vision is compelling, especially as they created it. But such leaders tend to lean toward an academic approach, intellectualizing and rationalizing the vision. Herein lies the trap. The vision becomes a complex and complicated model. And the original vision is lost somewhere along the way. It simply becomes invisible.

The first red flag comes when the leader opens the PowerPoint presentation. These sessions often begin well but somewhere around the fifth slide, I start to become restless. By the tenth slide it becomes uncomfortable, and by the fourteenth slide I've tuned out and simply wait for it to end. The question inevitably arises – what exactly is the vision?

Frankly speaking, if the leader can't summarize their vision in 60 seconds or less, it no longer qualifies as one. This is the true definition of the 'elevator pitch.' The game-changing leader must have the ability to deliver a high-impact message that is laser sharp, digestible – and, most important, memorable – by the time the team reaches the tenth floor.

The truth is, most CEOs, and senior leaders for that matter, need help with creating the vision. This is not to say that these leaders are not visionary. They are. But they struggle with the challenge of creating the vision in a way that can be expressed to the teams they lead – something that captures the true essence of their view of the future direction.

Now, here's the trick. The compelling vision is not so much about the 'what' as it is about the 'why.' 'Why' is where the trigger is pulled to make the vision a reality. The 'why' is what ensures your vision stays focused, sharp and meaningful. The 'why' prevents the vision from getting diluted and ultimately lost on your people. Because, when all is said and done, let's remember why we created the vision in the first place: to inspire action with purpose. The output, the business results, the measurable outcomes of our efforts then become proof of concept. A solid vision, with a strongly rooted purpose, sets the team up for success.

Henry Ford, the founder of Ford Motor Company and a captain of industry, had a unique ability to illustrate the 'why' in a powerful manner. His vision went beyond the cars he manufactured. He was the first to implement a minimum wage for the working man on the factory floor. And why was this minimum wage so important for Ford? He didn't consider it as a tool that would allow the worker on the assembly line to raise his standard of life. For Ford, it represented the opportunity for his workers to, one day, purchase the very car – the Model T – that they were building every day. Henry Ford's vision was to democratize the automobile, by making his car accessible to anyone who really wanted it. And therein he was creating a virtuous cycle, a community of Ford loyalists.

The Model T was thus conceived as a durable and affordable vehicle that the common man could own. He increased wages to the point where the assembly-line worker could afford to purchase the car. And through it, he provided his legion of employees with a new sense of freedom that inspired and gave them the opportunity to explore. He activated the curiosity of his workforce, which ultimately made Ford an innovator for decades to come. And, this vision resulted in a measurable return as attrition dropped significantly, further helping Ford's revenues to grow.

We can find some wonderful examples of vision statements all around us. The truly impactful ones have something in common. They paint a picture of the future, of what the world could – or perhaps better yet – *should* look like. The powerful vision does just that – it *envisions*. It addresses the greater *why* in a simple manner. It paints a crystal-clear picture. And these visions touch the hearts and minds, leaving no doubt.

Here are some famous examples:
- "Our vision is a world without Alzheimer's." This vision of the Alzheimer's Association cuts straight to the purpose. There is no need to debate on the 'why.' There is no room for misunderstanding or misinterpretation.
- "A computer on every desk, and in every home." Bill Gates was profound in his vision for Microsoft, but he then needed to demonstrate why this vision was important and the impact it could have on the world.
- "Spread ideas," says TED, and it does exactly that.
- IKEA's showrooms bring alive their vision: "To create a better everyday life for many people."

43

- Nordstrom's sales associates and design teams have a unique way of bringing their vision to life: "To give customers the most compelling shopping experience possible."
- Every Amazon employee takes the extra effort to fulfil Bezos' vision: "To be the Earth's most customer-centric company."
- Tesla appeals to the environmentalist in their employees and customers when they say, "To accelerate the world's transition to sustainable energy."
- Finally, Nike has firmly ensconced themselves as a champion in "bringing inspiration and innovation to every athlete in the world."

FIND **YOUR PURPOSE**

The purpose-centric and purpose-driven vision makes the biggest impact. Unless a leader's vision is solidly supported by values, no complex, profound or fancy vision will reach the minds and hearts of the team. Nor will it inspire action. It's all about your 'why,' your greater purpose. This is where your personal values enter the discussion.

In times of crisis, we discover the true character of the leader. This is true in times of war and tragedy. When there is fear, where there is peril or doubt, the strong leader steps up. Leaders must possess clear and positive values that are aligned with those of their organization. Only then can they rise to 'walk their talk.' Leaders must stand for something in order to achieve greatness. If we look at game-changing leaders throughout history and across genres, we find one common theme. These leaders had conviction rooted in something they strongly believed to be important. And they held firm in their beliefs – even when people doubted or mocked them. The leader with strong personal values, which align with those of the organization, becomes a pillar of purpose. It's this pillar that keeps the teams together through good times and bad.

Bill Hewlett and David Packard proved the immense power of values when they founded Hewlett Packard (HP). Their vision statement went like this:

"Our vision is to create technology that makes life better for everyone, everywhere – every person, every organization and every community around the globe. This motivates us – inspires us – to do what we do. To make what we make. To invent and to reinvent. To engineer experiences that amaze. We won't stop pushing ahead, because you won't stop pushing ahead. You're reinventing how you work. How you play. How you live. With our technology, you'll reinvent your world. This is our calling. This is a new HP. Keep reinventing."

'The HP Way' was thus born. The HP Way wasn't conceived as a business plan. Its big goal was not about the destination. Rather, it represented the personal core values of Bill Hewlett and David Packard. These values became the heart and soul of the company and the spirit is evident in their shared personal beliefs:
- First: the passion to make a technical contribution
- Second: the demand of superior performance – of itself as an organization and of its people

- Third: the belief that the best results come with the right people
- Fourth: the responsibility to contribute to the wellbeing of the communities in which they operate
- Fifth: integrity

The HP Way envisioned 'contribution' as the cornerstone of the company's existence. The critical question was "What can we contribute?" rather than "How can we succeed?" But the expectation was always that of stellar performance. And perhaps a core reason for their success was the belief that building a high-performing team begins with the notion, "First who, then what." It's interesting that Jim Collins in *Good to Great* identified this common characteristic among the long list of leading companies that he and his team investigated. It was that these companies were driven by leaders who put a high priority on getting the right people on the bus and creating an environment where these team members could thrive and achieve. In the process, high performance became the new normal.

In Dan Roam's book, *The Back of the Napkin*,[4] he talks about how sometimes the most interesting ideas, which then evolve into a compelling vision, are best crafted on the back of a napkin. A good example is Herb Kelleher and Rollin King at Southwest Airlines, who outlined a three-pillared strategy to carve out their unique space in a very crowded industry. They asked themselves the same question that game-changing leaders regularly pose to their teams: "How can we solve this problem?"

The result? Direct flights between the underserviced corridor of Dallas, Houston and San Antonio. And to imagine that this pioneering business model of Southwest Airlines was launched on the back of a napkin! Of course, the emphasis on warm and personal service for a reasonable price followed, and they identified the 'what.' And then changed the game by adding a very special 'how.'

Any leader who has sat with a colleague or team member in a café has at one time reached for a napkin, pulled out a pen and drawn a sketch of how things *should be*. This then typically leads to an engaging conversation of what *could be*. And by the time the coffee cup is empty, the writings on the napkin become a treasure of sorts, carefully folded, placed in the pocket, and brought up to the office to be crafted into a game-changing vision, or to simply end up in the wastebasket. When was the last time you sat in a café or a restaurant and crafted your own grand vision for yourself or your team?

Speaking of cafés and restaurants brings another example to my mind: ice cream! "We make the best possible ice cream in the best possible way." What a powerful statement! Ben Cohen and Jerry Greenfield didn't see themselves as starting an ice cream company. For them, making great ice cream provided the vehicle to bring joy to customers and make a positive impact on the world. Their statement "Peace, Love and Ice Cream" is completely aligned with their sense of purpose and values. They were using ice cream to create a movement. And with each scoop of the ever-popular strawberry cheesecake or chocolate chip cookie dough flavours, they took one more step forward to change the world.

It's common practice in recent years for organizations to conduct engagement surveys of their employees. These surveys can offer some revealing insights and are a good way for leaders to capture the pulse of the organization. One discovery from these surveys is that the engagement score, and the subsequent performance of the team, is directly connected with the rating employees give to the following statements: "I have faith in my leadership team and the strategy that they've created," and "The direction of the organization is clear and meaningful."

It's surprising to see so many employees (and managers) who are unclear about the strategy and the greater purpose of why their organizations exist. It's not surprising, therefore, that these organizations typically underperform against the benchmarks of growth and market standing. The knockout punch for these lagging organizations is a commonly heard statement: "I don't think my leader really knows where they are going."

Let's be fair. Even the most exceptional leaders will agree that while they may have a crystal-clear vision and full commitment to bring it to life, what they can't predict are the twists and turns that lie ahead on the journey. They begin with the assumption that challenges will come along, and unpredictability awaits them throughout the journey. As the bumps in the road emerge, strong leaders send out a clear message through their words and behaviours that the team is on the right path. This sense of conviction from the leader and the belief it creates in times of doubt is extremely powerful, and it's what differentiates the competent manager from the game-changing leader.

THE POWER OF **PURPOSE**

In March 2011, Japan was hit by an earthquake in the Tohoku region. But it was the tsunami that followed that shook the nation to its core. In a land where earthquakes are a regular occurrence, the country had not seen a tragedy of this magnitude and with such devastating impact for decades. More than 22,000 lives were lost, and entire towns vanished in the tsunami.

I was in Japan for the Kobe earthquake in 1995, and experienced its horror and devastation first-hand. Earthquakes like the ones that struck Kobe and Tohoku, both at 7+ on the Richter scale, are massive. These earthquakes were especially violent; it literally shook to the core. The aftershocks continue for months and it's no surprise that so many residents of Kobe still suffer from PTSD nearly 25 years later.

Immediately following the earthquake and tsunami in 2011, the Japanese women's soccer team had to make a very difficult decision – whether to participate in the FIFA World Cup tournament or to honour the victims of the tragedy by staying home. After much discussion and soul-searching, and with full support from the families of the deceased, the team travelled to Germany for the competition, just three months after the tragedy.

Nobody gave the Japanese team a chance of winning. Like most teams in Asia, while they were known for their speed and persistence, their skill was seen as well below the powerhouse teams from the US and Germany. But the women from Japan were on a mission. They arrived in Europe, committed to represent their nation, and bring some bit of joy and comfort to Japan that was so saddened by the recent horrible tragedy. Their coach, Norio Sasaki, felt it was the right decision to travel to Germany and compete. And in the two days leading up to their first match, instead of giving the team an inspirational pump-up speech, he decided to do something different. He turned down the lights and showed photos of the after-effects of the tsunami, the scenes of devastation and the faces of the survivors. He didn't need to say a word; the images struck deep in the soul of every single player on the team.

What came next was perhaps one of the greatest moments in sports history. Ten million fans in Japan, from the northern tip of Hokkaido to the southern islands of Okinawa – and tens of millions more around the world – watched the Japanese women pull off what could be called a miracle, when they defeated the US team on penalties. It was this fierce sense of purpose and belief that helped propel a team of average talent to World Cup victory. The team's nickname, 'Nadeshiko,' was named after a pink flower that symbolizes classic Japanese beauty. The flower also represents resilience, a fitting symbol for this remarkable team of women.

Hope Solo, the legendary American goalkeeper who sustained an injury in the final game against Japan, commented after the upset loss. "They're playing for something bigger and better than the game," Solo said.[5] "When you're playing with so much emotion, that's hard to play against."

The Nadeshiko were on a mission. They believed they could do the unthinkable, they rallied together and then they went out and did it.

DEFINING SUCCESS. PAINTING A PICTURE OF WHAT IT LOOKS LIKE.

THE GAME-CHANGING LEADER, THEN, IS A VISION-CRAFTER.

When it comes to **envision**, we know that game-changing leaders recognize its importance. They spend considerable time and effort to craft a vision that will serve as a guide to take the team to the day after tomorrow. Game-changing leaders choose to *pursue greatness.*

Now it's your turn to craft your own vision. Let's begin by asking some important questions:

- Does the vision talk about the future?
- Does the vision talk about why we exist?
- Is the vision human and authentic?
- Does the vision talk about what's in it for the team?
- Does the vision touch the hearts and minds of your people?
- Does the vision appeal at the core to all team members?
- Is the vision sharp and easy to digest?
- Is the vision elevator-proof?

While the output and the exchange of the different versions of the future is a lot of fun and a great energizing activity, it also provides some valuable insight for you as the leader. It's a pulse check on how well the team has digested your vision, and how strong their belief is that it's achievable. Once the vision is shared with the group, the discussion inevitably shifts gears toward "How will we make this a reality?"

But before we dive into the 'how', it's crucial to address the 'why.'

And so, the bold and compelling vision has been created. We now move to the next step – the 'why.' Why are we going to do this? Why is it important to have a world without Alzheimer's?

VISIONARY LEADERS ARE DREAMERS. AND THEY ARE EVEN STRONGER WHEN THEY DREAM TOGETHER WITH THEIR TEAMS.

Why is it important to eliminate cancer from this planet? Why is it important for us to spread new ideas? Asking 'why' ignites reflection and curiosity. Every person on your team has their own unique buttons, the motivators that inspire them to action. Psychometric tests reveal various personality types and multitudes of combinations. There is the 'mile-long and inch-deep' profile who is excited by overall concepts, but not by their miniscule details. You also have the analytical and reflective member who wants to know more about the deeper meaning of the vision. And there are varying shades in between.

So, how do you craft a vision that reflects your passion, which also pushes the right buttons across such a diverse demography? It begins by asking yourself this question: "What will get my team off their chairs and inspired to action?"

Whenever I go into a new situation or an unfamiliar environment as a leader, the first thing I do is pause to observe and learn. There is a great phrase in Japanese that says, "Read the air in the room (*kuuki wo yomu*)." It means being very aware of the body language, relationships between team members and the silence between the words, which speak volumes. More simply put, it means you need to stop and observe.

S.T.O.P.

I first learned the importance of taking the time to observe back in my teenage days as a Canadian army cadet. Thanks to the persistent encouragement of my commanding officer, I had an amazing opportunity to be part of a military version of Outward Bound. We spent seven weeks in survival training at Camp Petawawa, deep in the rugged forests and lakes of northern Ontario. During that summer, we were placed in high-stress situations with a high level of unpredictability, called missions. In one instance, we had just retired from an extremely rigorous four-day orienteering trek through the dense bush. That night, physically and mentally worn out from the challenge, we were relieved to be able to crawl into the comfort of our tents and a warm sleeping bag for a good night's sleep.

But our solace was abruptly and loudly interrupted at 3am when our tents were suddenly ripped down, and we were rolled off our cots by our platoon officers. As they kicked our cots and repeatedly blew their whistles, the command was loud and clear. "You have three minutes to get dressed in your combat gear, head-to-toe and into formation," was the order. "Failure to do so, and you will be RTB-ed (army lingo for 'return to base,' the equivalent of being disqualified) … go go go!!"

All 20 members of our platoon made it to the line-up just in time. As we stood shoulder to shoulder in the darkness, our officers ordered us to be silent, then they proceeded to move behind us and tie large blindfolds over each of our heads, covering our entire face. The instructions from our Master Warrant Officer then went as follows:

"You will now commence Mission Solo. For the next three days, you will be placed in an unfamiliar terrain, alone. You will be issued these items – an empty water bottle, a ground-sheet, ten feet of string, a whistle, a jackknife, three matches, a pencil and a notebook … and six squares of toilet paper."

As much as we wanted to chuckle at the last items, none of us dared risking being RTB-ed.

He then went on to explain our orders. "You will be dropped off one by one in the bush. You are to stay in that location, keep your blindfold on, count down from 100; when you reach zero, remove the blindfold. From that point, your operation zone is limited to a circumference of 30 steps in any direction from that spot where you were dropped. You are banned from moving beyond this drop zone. From this moment onward you are not to speak to another person during these three days. If you violate any of these conditions, you will be returned to mommy (the alternative version of RTB). If you have an emergency or feel the need to give up, blow the whistle that has been provided repeatedly in three sharp bursts. Welcome to Mission Solo."

We stood there in total silence as a large army transport truck pulled up on the dirt road where we waited in the night. We climbed up one by one, sat on the bench, blindfolded, still groggy and nervous about the mission ahead. The truck forged ahead into the trail, normally used as a logging road. As we bumped up and down for 20 minutes, the truck came to a halt and the commander yelled, "Northrop … go!" I could hear my tent mate and good buddy jump from the truck, hit the dirt, and in total silence we drove off into the forest. After a few more stops, my heart jumped at the sound of "Dupuis … go!" I shuffled to the edge of the truck and the officer pushed me into the night. Our training kicked in, and as I landed, I rolled on my side and came to a crouch in the brush, listening as the truck drove away with the remaining members of my platoon onboard.

Then the countdown began from 100 ... 99 ... 98 ... when I reached zero, I remove the blindfold. And this is when a very important classroom session on survival we had a few weeks earlier flashed back.

Our Master Warrant Officer taught us that when you face a tough, highly stressful situation, the first thing to ensure survival is to activate the **STOP response**: Stop, Think, Observe, Plan.

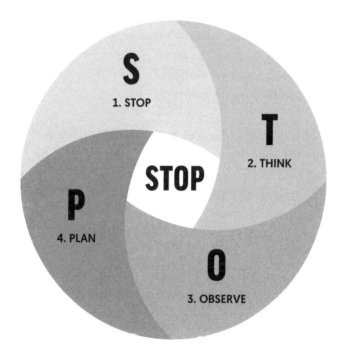

S – Stop. Take a deep breath, collect yourself and your thoughts; no action, simply stop and get your mind and body in a calm place.

T – Think. Give thought to the situation, repeat the current situation you face in your head, define it, get clarity on the reality.

O – Observe. Look around you, the environment, the people, the mood, take the temperature.

P – Plan. Based on what you've seen, take your thoughts and begin to create a plan. Identify possible scenarios, write them down, evaluate the possible outcomes, cause and effect. Choose your option and prepare for action. Most importantly, expect the best and prepare for the worst.

Now, in your own organization, it's probably not a good idea to blindfold your team members and leave them in the jungle without food and water for three days! But the STOP framework has relevance for all leaders who are facing a tough challenge. It aligns especially well with the common practice of new leaders who typically create a 30-, 60- or 90-day plan. The first 30 days should be all about meeting people, asking questions, and listening more than speaking. This enables you, as the new leader, to understand the positive elements from the past. It's important to protect the good stuff and then build on it with your own ideas.

The phrase, 'two ears and one mouth' is especially important in this phase. When you do that, you gather insight on the key buttons, the words that motivate people on your team, and inspire them to action. We discover these words by first *listening* for them.

CHAPTER 3 - ENVISION

As experienced marketers will tell you, ask a diverse group of people the same question and you'll start to see a pattern emerge. The pattern of responses become valid pulse checks of the current status of the organization. And when you begin to observe the behaviours that go with them, the opportunity for change becomes increasingly clear.

And here's an interesting discovery. In most cases, the answers to most of your questions are right there in the room. When you ask people what motivates them, they will give you generic vanilla answers. But if you begin to use their language, and ask the most basic questions, digging deeper each time, the discoveries can be valuable ingredients for your vision to follow.

Ask the important questions:
- What do you see as the key strategic priorities of the company right now?
- And for your team?
- Why did you join this company?
- Why do you stay?
- What would make you leave?

Then move on to questions like:
- When do you feel most energized as part of the organization?
- When do you get frustrated?

When you start to see a pattern emerge both in terms of repeated responses as well as differences, you're one step closer to the 'plan' stage. This would normally come between 60–90 days. Once the plan is clear, the next step is to take action.

"WHEN YOU TALK, YOU'RE ONLY REPEATING WHAT YOU ALREADY KNOW. BUT IF YOU LISTEN, YOU MAY LEARN SOMETHING NEW."

THE DALAI LAMA

Whether you lead a large complex organization, with a variety of roles and personalities across locations, or a smaller team in one location, the challenge is the same. Everyone in the room is motivated by something. The leader searches for the common thread as they weave their story. And here is a profound truth: the common thread usually isn't connected with goals or outcomes. It comes from the greater purpose, the very reason that we exist.

For example, let's imagine that I stand in front of my team and colleagues from several offices in India and focus my talk on profitability. Without a doubt, I will immediately lose the attention and engagement of a big segment of my audience. But let's say I choose to talk about teamwork. Or about rewards and recognition. I'm sure I'll touch the chords of most of the people in front of me. If teamwork is a core value of the organization, it should appeal to most people in the room. And if it doesn't, then I should be asking myself the tough question: "Is that person the right fit for my organization? Should they be on our bus?"

You could argue that everyone in the organization should be motivated by delivering profit. But in reality, it's not necessarily the case. Remember, profit is an outcome of doing the right things, living the values of the organization, which are in sync with the personal values of the leader. In my case, I'm especially passionate about transparency, resilience, teamwork, humility and good ethics. I talk about these values with my teams every chance I get and draw a connection between our behaviours and the outcomes we generate.

The game-changing leader brings a vision that touches the hearts and minds of everyone on the team. That's not an easy task, especially when there is team diversity. But what we know for sure is that organizations that embrace diversity are stronger. Diversity in gender, backgrounds, abilities and ways of seeing the world – this combination is formidable. At the same time, crafting a vision which speaks to and touches such a diverse group is a daunting challenge. It's no wonder that many managers fall into the 'mini-me syndrome,' unconsciously (or consciously), hiring people just like themselves. We've all seen the limitations that a team full of 'yes people' brings: mediocrity and potential disaster.

And so, we come back to values. Let's take a closer look at the mission of the Alzheimer's Association: "The Association has a vision of a world without the terrible emotional and physical pain that Alzheimer's causes the sufferer and their families." Now, if you have no personal experience with Alzheimer's, this vision may not impact you as much as someone who has felt the pain and frustration first-hand. On the other hand, there are many people who work for and passionately support the association, although they've never been directly impacted by the disease.

What does this tell us? The vision of the Alzheimer's Association pushes an important human button that is universal in nature, regardless of culture, demographics and personality profile. That is, to bring an end to suffering of any kind. We can all relate to this because at one time in our lives, we have all suffered. This is especially important when we move to the next E – **express**.

It's important to use the right language in crafting your vision. The core message should be less focused on outcomes, and more about *why* we exist. In the case of the Alzheimer's Association, the vision implies that the suffering caused by the disease is bad, and that we must do something about it. When it's hard to argue with the 'why', the 'how' will naturally follow.

Let's imagine you're standing in front of a team of salespeople. By the very nature of the role, salespeople are motivated by the hunt, the spirit of competition and being recognized and rewarded for achieving their targets. Where many leaders go wrong, however, is adjusting the message on their vision to be solely about achieving targets and receiving a hefty incentive reward. While this may be a key motivator for the salesperson, it should be expressed as an outcome of working toward the vision, living and breathing the core values and using their unique skill set to help the organization achieve the collective goal. The leader needs to use language that pushes the buttons of the salesperson and ignites the spark to action. It should be clear that 'winning' and receiving a big paycheck are outcomes of achieving the vision, but these do not equate to the vision.

What happens then, when the leader is addressing the risk and compliance team? The auditor sees the world through very different lenses than the salesperson does. The paycheck may motivate them, but it's not the number-one motivational button. For the person who is passionate about managing risk and ensuring the organization is compliant, financial targets are an outcome of doing the right things. Their focus is on the 'how' as the guardians of the organization, and they live by the mantra of 'protect and enable.' But let's be clear: being compliant with the law of the land and company standards should not be the sole objective. This team needs to understand that by keeping the organization on the 'right side,' they are playing a key role in helping the organization achieve a greater purpose and, ultimately, to enable the vision to become a reality.

As we saw in the 2008 global financial crisis, many banks were smashing their financial targets, delivering returns to shareholders and earning large sums for their managers. You could say that the salespeople had outperformed, and therefore achieved the expectations placed on them by the company. However, as they discovered the hard way, their achievement came at the expense of compliance and ethics. Their wins resulted in someone else's losses. The 'bad profits' in the end caused these organizations to crumble. Imagine the outcome if they had worked closely with their risk and compliance teams, taken their advice and were guided by a shared vision, with an emphasis on values and behaviours. It's safe to say that this devastating crisis could have been then avoided. I would even venture to say that plenty of money could still have been made. The difference is that this would have been 'good money.' But without a clear vision, a greater purpose, a compelling why, or the right guiding principles, the chance of swerving in the wrong direction is high.

If you're starting to feel like **envision** is more complicated than you originally thought, you're right. But the good news is that there are some very effective strategies to help you craft a vision that is game-changing.

When we look at the most impactful leaders from business, sports, the arts and beyond, we see a common behaviour related to how they regard time. These leaders are extremely selfish and protective of their time. They view it as an asset, a weapon of sorts, which fuels the effort to bring the vision to reality. Robin Sharma, in his book, *The 5 AM Club*,[6] discovered something very interesting about how high performers manage their time. Or perhaps a better way to say it is how they *leverage* their time. In his encounters with high-performing professional athletes, actors, entrepreneurs, CEOs and elected politicians, he discovered a common theme – they all place a premium on time. In fact, one insightful 'coincidence' he observed was that true game changers typically wake up early (hence the name of the book!). More specifically, he was surprised to find that a large number of them wake up at 5am. They also went to bed early, typically by 10pm. The old mantra of "early to bed and early to rise leads to a long life" could be adjusted to read "early to bed, early to rise brings impact."

Leaders should understand the importance of the need to make and carve out time – to collect their thoughts, contemplate, and climb out of the daily grind. And they know that this reflection time and the moments when to turn off must be protected at all costs.

It's often said that strategy is about seeing the world from 30,000 feet. I would argue that the leader who spends most of his time at 30,000 feet is likely to be out of touch with what's happening on the ground. And, let's face it, the real action is on the ground. The ones who actually move the needle are the frontline soldiers, the middle managers, the players. The further the leader is away from the ground, the less connected that leader becomes with reality. As a result, their ability to make decisions based on authentic and accurate perspectives is weakened. At the critical stage of creating a North Star for the organization, it's imperative that the leader has a clear grip on the pulse of the team – and how can they do that from 30,000 feet, far out of sight and reach of the people who will bring the vision to life?

So, it's important for the leader to move back and forth from the mud, the micro of the day-to-day activity, then up to 100 feet, to view the landscape, the progress along with the opportunities and threats. Knowing when to position yourself on the ground and high above is an important quality of a game-changing leader.

This ability to know when to be with the team on the floor and in the field, versus locked up in the boardroom planning strategy with senior leaders, is a leadership muscle. Like any muscle, it can be developed over time. And through practice, this becomes a reflexive ability. In fact, in recent years, there is considerable research around the idea that leadership is less science and more weighted toward art. As such, a leader's soft skills and EQ become more important than the hard technical skills and domain knowledge. It's interesting that most of the books on leadership, used in MBA programmes and beyond, are focused on the mechanics of leadership, with a heavy emphasis on the leadership algorithm. When, in fact, we have come to realize that leadership is an ability and a sense that is developed through trial and error.

In the book, *Reflexive Leadership*,[7] Mats Alvesson et al. talk about how leadership is no longer something that leaders *do*. In other words, leadership is not a task, but a vocation. It's a journey, and it becomes innate over time, to the point that when a seasoned leader faces a challenge, they respond in a purely reflexive manner. But where does that leadership reflex come from? Like all reflexes, it's born out of our experiences, from our successes and failures, and refined through reflections.

I discovered this thing called 'leadership reflex' many years ago. It came after a particularly bad decision I made as a leader, one that ultimately caused the team, which I had worked so hard to build, to crumble. I made the decision to hire someone as the manager of a key team, based on the strong recommendation of my boss, when I knew that this wasn't the right person for us. I had spent additional time interviewing this person and had seen the warning signs, while my manager was urging me to make a decision based on a recommendation from a friend. In hindsight, if I had gone with my instinctive response (aka my reflex), I wouldn't have made the hire and I'm sure the team would have continued to thrive. I realized then that I needed to not only trust my instinct but to build muscles around my leadership reflex, so that when the next challenge arose, I'd be sharp and ready to make the best decision for that moment. And to stand up and push back when the reflex says "no."

I find perspective when I take long walks, sometimes alone and sometimes with colleagues. There is something special that happens when we move the body and the mind simultaneously. Any long-distance runner or cyclist will tell you that being

GAME-CHANGING LEADERS LOOK IN THE MIRROR.

THEY SEEK THE TRUTH, AND THEN THEY DEAL WITH IT.

'in the zone' brings a sense of calm, and often a sort of enlightenment. Marathoners call it the 'runner's high.' It's a state of clarity, when the body and mind are functioning together in a zone. But the same runners will also tell us that it takes time to get into that zone. In fact, for many marathon runners, the zone doesn't appear until the 10km mark. I find my zone when I'm at the gym or pedalling away in the early morning through the side streets of India on my mountain bike. As I pump off the reps, physically I'm in the game but mentally my mind will wander and think about big questions like, "What if we … ?" and "How could I have handled the issue that I faced yesterday better?" And right around the 10th rep or the 15th km, when I conclude that I could've done better, I find myself pumping three or four more reps with intensity. My personal trainer gets a kick out of the fact that when he says, "C'mon, two more reps Paul!," I usually shoot for four or five more. Eager leaders always aim to take things beyond expectations (and pay for it the next day!).

In my interactions with leaders, there is a clear pattern between performance and the level of introspection of the leader. The leaders who make an impact understand that in order to keep their leadership sword sharp, it's important to continuously look in the mirror, and reflect on their own behaviours and responses to specific challenges. Sometimes the conclusion might be "I can do better." At other times, the conclusion may be "I handled it just right." It's not about second-guessing oneself, it's more about reaffirmation, a check-up on the leadership reflex.

The game-changing leader embraces the *process*. Whether you put those ideas down on paper, or type them straight onto your tablet,

or simply verbalize them, it's a healthy thing to do. Some leaders I
know record their thoughts on their smartphone's voice recorder.
In fact, that's how I started to craft this book. It began with
hundreds of audio files that I recorded, out on my balcony, coffee
mug in hand, thinking out loud the random thoughts. I began
with answering these questions: "Why am I writing this book?"
"What do I want the readers to take away from the book?" "How
can I stay focused and aligned through this process?"

Regardless of the medium you use, self-conversations are a healthy
approach to help your ideas take shape, to make sense of, to filter
and, in the process, identify the key ingredients that will make up
your vision. As the ideas move to execution, the levels of passion
and ownership inevitably lead to unparalleled momentum. And
once the team owns it, once they are convinced that they have the
answers to a problem, it's an opportunity for the leader to simply
step back and allow it to happen. The move from *stepping up* to
stepping back is a key trait of the leader as enabler.

It was in one of my moments of quiet reflection that I hit upon
the idea of the *Shark Tank*. I had watched a few episodes of this
popular TV show that weekend – and was struck by the manner
in which budding entrepreneurs creatively presented their ideas
to hard-nosed investors. They had a script but were also ready
to ad-lib and make on-the-spot, ad hoc decisions – pivoting to
capture the support they desperately wanted.

Imagine if our own teams behaved like the people making
their pitches in *Shark Tank*. To bring creative solutions – and
more importantly – to own them. That was a very ambitious

VISIONARY LEADERS ASK THEMSELVES AND THEIR TEAMS A VERY IMPORTANT QUESTION:

"WHAT ARE WE MISSING HERE?"

undertaking for an organization that had traditionally approached problem solving – with the boss having all the answers! I wanted to flip the whole paradigm upside down. And so we launched our own version of *Shark Tank*. The concept is simple: we take a business challenge or an opportunity (it can be internal or external), create diverse teams of people – representing the front, middle and back offices, and from multiple geographies – who normally would not work together. Each team is issued the same challenge, with the same context setting and supporting data points. And then the challenge is issued – come up with a solution. In just three hours they have to define the problem, clarify the opportunity and possible outcomes in fixing it, the benefits for the organization, and what success would look like. And finally, of course, the 'how' of making it happen.

The beauty of the shark tank model is that in the process of conducting it, you'll discover that the answers are always in the room. More importantly, the teams themselves realize *they have the answers*. We've had some incredible ideas come out of this initiative in the organizations I've led - and quite a few of them have proven to be game changers. Go ahead and give your 'sharks' a chance!

In order to ignite teams to action, leaders need to ask questions that challenge and prompt to action:

What are we missing?
The nature of this question suggests something that every successful leader knows well. We are *always* missing something. If your team is going to make the leap from underperforming

to outperforming, leaders must constantly challenge the status quo. And once the team feels dissatisfaction with the current status quo, the seeds of transformation are born. And while things may be going well, the trigger to take the organization from bad to good – and from good to great – is often not a radical change but instead a tweak of things already in place. In some cases, what's missing is the most critical element of **envision** – a crystal-clear North Star, the greater purpose.

Which way is north?

By 2017, after 22 years in Japan, I had built a certain degree of credibility. And over time I had erased most of my blind spots. I knew how to build high-performing teams, how to mobilize and how to get things done in the country.

And then I arrived in India. On many levels, my leadership ability was about to face the ultimate test. I was moving across borders and cultures into a complex and alien environment where I had no connections and no track record. And certainly, I had no understanding of the intricacies of the business climate and the people. I needed to get a clear idea of the direction in which my team was going or where they thought they were going.

So, I initiated something called the 'compass survey' – an anonymous survey of my leadership team. The survey was a simple pulse check to gain valuable insight into the minds of the leaders and to better understand the buttons that needed to be pushed to trigger a transformation.

Three key questions:
- What are the key strategic priorities for our organization this year?
- What should be our key strategic priorities?
- What's stopping us from accelerating forward toward our goals?

Teams that perform at a high level typically have a limited number of key priorities – ideally three or four, no more. Strong leaders focus on going narrow and deep in everything they do. In this particular case, 40 senior leaders across the company participated in the compass survey. When the responses were clustered, we discovered 17 uniquely different strategic priorities. In other words, we had a group of senior managers tasked with leading a large complex organization in multiple geographies, lines of business and support functions moving in 17 uniquely different directions. And here's the shocker – there was very little overlap in what they listed as strategic priorities. This was perhaps the most important revelation – no wonder the team was underperforming and showing little, if any, traction!

The answer to the question, "What am I missing?," was crystal clear. This was an organization in disarray, It was a team that lacked confidence, was siloed, fragmented and lacked a clear unifying goal. People did not know each other and, more importantly, they didn't trust each other. Teamwork was naturally missing – to the point of sabotage at times. Underlying all of this was a mixed bag of culture. And the outcomes reflected this clutter. No organization with such a high degree of divergence can expect high performance. Even if a team managed to deliver solid performance, it would neither be scalable nor sustainable.

We began by confronting the brutal facts. I showed the 17 answers, in which three factors consistently overlapped. It's no surprise that the three common focus areas were about achieving revenue budget, EBITA/profit target and year-on-year growth target. But all of this is what I affectionately call 'hygiene.' None of these goals were strategic, and certainly none were game-changing. And most importantly, none of these objectives had a greater purpose. I needed to help the leaders understand that achieving revenue, profit and growth targets should not be the end goal. Instead, greatness is achieved by having the right people, united in purpose, working together, aligned to a common strategy, guided by strong core values, and fully supported by committed leaders to make the vision become reality. This offsite was a huge step forward, as we planted the seeds of a culture of looking in the mirror, confronting the brutal facts, and rallying together to come up with a shared plan of action to get better.

Unfortunately, these negative traits are rather common in most underperforming organizations. Uncovering them is one thing; dismantling them is quite another. As the captain of this ship, I quickly came to appreciate the enormity of the challenge ahead. I realized that I had to do something about it immediately. This became my first priority.

From the words used in the responses to the compass survey, we created a word cloud. The size of the words in the cloud reflected how often they were used in the responses to other questions. It was then time to identify patterns to dig deeper on what the responses were telling us about the leadership team and identify key action items to get the ship on the right course.

I am not a big believer in the 'fun offsites.' You know, the ones where the facilitator has the groups play games that appear to be cleverly designed to illustrate a point related to teamwork or strategy. These are time fillers, and we didn't have the luxury of time. In this case, I needed our leaders to come together with a sense of urgency, not emergency. On a mission to dig deep on carving out our North Star, to find our shared purpose. And then make a commitment to act together to ensure it comes to life. We needed to get to work.

The compass offsite should be built around a specific theme and a clear objective. For an organization that is underperforming, with a lack of a shared strategy, the offsite should be focused on identifying the common purpose and direction. It's a significant investment of leaders' time, effort and money. Pulling leaders away from their teams can slow momentum, and so, the offsite must have measurable impact.

The compass meeting is an opportunity to create an environment where team members can be themselves, away from the bubble of the day-to-day grind. It's also a chance for the team to get to know each other, and you as their leader. It's your chance to share your observations and insights on what you've seen both in the current organization, and in your past experiences. In our case, this was the time to dig deep into the word cloud and the 17 strategic priorities that the leaders identified in their responses. Discussion, disagreement and debate were all part of this process.

It was our moment of collectively confronting the brutal facts. We acknowledged we were way too wide and shallow – with no common vision or goal – and certainly, we were not speaking a common language. On the other hand, we also acknowledged, admitted and identified the good things that were happening – and how we could leverage them into our vision and plans that would propel us to the day after tomorrow.

As part of cocreating the vision, we agreed on a number of things we would stop doing. We would stop being shallow and wide. Instead, we would plough in narrow and deep. We would not just rest at being a trusted partner for clients and candidates. We would become the most admired company in our industry.

This was a great start. But even as we closed in on what we needed to do, I came away from the meeting a little perplexed. How was I going to bring this team of very capable, strong-minded leaders, accustomed to a fragmented culture, to walk together arm in arm, and in one direction? That's when I began to walk myself.

Most game-changing leaders share two very similar habits. They're early risers – the alarm clocks of the most impactful leaders are set for 5am. And they walk a lot. This is when they think, brainstorm and craft the roots of their compelling visions. Steve Jobs was well known for his 'walking meetings,' and many of the breakthrough ideas that revolutionized Apple (and the world of technology, for that matter) were born on these walks.

Borrowing a page from the books of these leaders, I took long, early morning walks several times a week. On my morning walks, I thought out loud, asking myself the same questions I would ask the leaders on my team: "What is our greater purpose?" "What's holding us back?" Over time (and lots of steps), the answers started to emerge. We were too focused on the past, and this legacy culture was holding us back. We had a culture of blame, with a weak sense of accountability. And finally, we had a siloed culture where teamwork took a backseat to individual and team achievements. And so, our mantras were born: we honour the past and focus on the future. We look in the mirror and raise the bar. We are One Team; we win together.

Mantras are very powerful tools for leaders. They become your guiding principles, a lighthouse that helps give direction, especially useful in times of turmoil and disruption. Crafting mantras with a specific purpose is helpful – these help to build a strong culture around your vision. Your mantra then, is a guiding light. And from this, your vision is born.

The past is important, but I am convinced that the future is the priority. Your vision should include creating a future-thinking and a future-focused organization, a culture in which your team talks about tomorrow instead of yesterday.

The wonderful thing about leadership is that it's not only a science or an art, it's both. The art allows you to add your own personal and unique human touch. The science adds an element of predictability, a formula that can be replicated with a bit of tweaking depending on the particular leadership challenge you face.

THE WONDERFUL THING
ABOUT LEADERSHIP IS THAT
IT'S BOTH AN ART AND
A SCIENCE.

THE GAME-CHANGING
LEADER, THOUGH, WILL
NEVER BE REMEMBERED
FOR THE SCIENCE.

TIPS: ENVISION TO TOUCH THE MIND AND HEART

As with leadership itself, there is no one-size-fits-all formula for the process of envisioning. However, there are a few tips to help you along.

Your vision should be compelling, both in content and context.
It needs to touch both the heart and the mind.

Your vision should be laser sharp.
Nobody remembers a ten-page PowerPoint about the vision. Keep it short, sharp and memorable, with easy-to-digest simplicity.

Your vision should be inclusive.
It has to be attractive to anyone, regardless of their role and their views of the world. When expressed, the majority in the room should get it and be inspired to action.

Your vision should be bold.
Inspiration to action is sparked by ambition, not by protecting the status quo. Be bold and craft a vision to change the world.

It's a tall order, no doubt. So, how do leaders get their initial ideas for a vision? Sometimes the inspiration comes by accident, like Archimedes with his 'Eureka' moment in a bathtub. Legend has it that he shouted, "Eureka!" in an 'aha' moment of understanding the relationship between the volume of water displaced to the volume of the body submerged.

Just like Archimedes, many leaders literally get their inspiring moments in the shower. For others, the breakthrough idea may come in the middle of the night (if that's you, I suggest you keep a notebook and a pen by your bed). A few others, me included, find their bulbs burning the brightest on long walks – that's when my own 'aha' moments seem to come.

Meditation, reading, reflecting … these are all opportunities to think and discover. Which is your idea generator? Find your source and make time for it. You'll be surprised by the discoveries that naturally emerge.

Now that we have a fair idea about the key ingredients of a vision, and you've committed to find your own source of inspiration, what do we do when an idea strikes us? Capture it immediately as is, no filters required. You'll have plenty of time to think about and analyse it later. And when you do, think about its meaning and purpose. Does the answer to your 'what if?' question excite you? Does it scare you? Does it inspire you to action? If the answer is yes to these questions, you're on the right track. Develop your idea, polish it, and just imagine what will happen when your team shares your excitement and embraces your vision.

When I first came to India, I set out on a mission to visit my teams across the four corners of the country. This roadshow, as we called it, was an opportunity to get my fingers on the pulse of the people in my organization. It took a lot to resist the urge to tell rather than listen. But I held myself to the mantra that guided me in these conversations – two ears and one mouth!

After a brief self-introduction and greetings to the team, I was consistently asked the same question wherever I went, and by team members regardless of their role or level. "So, Paul, what is your vision for the organization in India?"

And I had the same answer for everyone. "My first vision is to understand you, the history, our people, and our current situation. We can then look at the future. So, you can hear about my vision in the next 60 days." I kept this message on track to build the suspense and engagement of the people. In the course of doing so, I changed the narrative from '*my vision*' to '*our vision*.' Cocreating the vision was the mantra.

And here is an important insight in the process of creating a vision. People are quick to assume that the leader will lock himself in a room and come up with an amazing vision to guide the organization to great heights. Nothing could be further from reality. The best vision, like strategy, should be co-created with the people who will lead its execution. In fact, the leader doesn't necessarily need to be the oracle that unleashes the vision. An organization that has had a frequent change in leaders over a period of time may be better suited for bottom-up vision crafting. This approach requires the top leader to be in the game and connected.

Leadership is tough. And it's easy to point out after the fact whether a particular leader brought the right leadership to a particular organization. In reality, it's not about being right or wrong, it's about making an impact. Leaders, by the very nature of 'stepping up' to the challenge, are part of a special fraternity. And if you're a leader of people, you have my admiration.

Unfortunately, many of us begin each leadership challenge by minimizing, criticizing or even dismissing the previous leader. I recommend a different approach that has served me well. That is, to 'honour the past, and focus on the future.'

Bringing your vision alive is as critical, as demanding and as challenging as getting it on your drawing board and fleshing it out. Here is where, as a leader, you bring your versatile communication and relationship-building capabilities into play.

Bold. Authentic. Impactful. Simple. Inclusive. These are all key traits of a powerful vision. It helps to begin by asking yourself these questions:

- Why are you crafting this vision?
- What do you hope to achieve with this vision?
- How invested are you, as the leader, in it?
- Where do you, as their leader, want to take the company and the people?
- How does the vision reveal the values of the organization?
- What will the world look like when the vision is brought to life?
- What will the journey be like?
- How do we get to where we want to be?
- What role does each member of the team play in the ambition?

When you're faced with a leadership challenge, begin by asking yourself these questions. It's good to have your laptop or tablet with you or, for the old school leaders out there like me, grab a pen and a notebook. Write down your ideas, reflect, walk away. Come back, revisit, trim, polish. Over time, your vision will gradually emerge, and start to take shape. This is when the fun begins.

One word of caution. When you unveil the vision, be prepared that your vision might not touch or engage everyone in the room. This is to be expected because not all visions are for everyone. So, when you craft your vision, be aware that tough choices will need to be made, which will test the mettle of your leadership. You may conclude that while your vision is rock solid, you may be surrounded by people who can't, or simply won't, work together with you to bring the vision to life. We'll deal with that later in the book when we get into the **express** and **excite** phases.

For me, 'One team, we win together' was at the core of how I approached my vision. I began spreading this message wherever I went. In town halls. In leadership team meetings. In my one-to-one chats over coffee with colleagues. In fact, at every touchpoint, the spirit of 'one team' emerged. We began to recognize those who lived this value, and each time we repeated the message of why it's important.

Over time, an interesting thing happened – evangelists started to emerge and my message began to gain momentum. And, in a surprising way, it started to take a life of its own. I knew we had touched a nerve when I came out of a leadership team meeting one morning to see cardboard standees on every desk in the office.

My messages had evolved into what would become our mantras:

Honour the Past, Focus on the Future.
Look in the Mirror, Raise the Bar.
One Team, We Win Together.

Our marketing team had taken the initiative to reach out to the IT team to come up with a plan to share the message using their own creative channels. They placed these standees simultaneously on every desk of every employee across our locations in 25 cities in India. The IT team came through on this too … every desktop had the same wallpaper. It was an omnichannel visual display of what we believed in and held close to us. The message had arrived to the four corners of India and the organization.

The mantra of, **'One team, we win together'** had made the leap from being a dream conceived on a walk in the park, evolving into a mantra that helped guide us forward.

As you craft your own compelling vision, come up with some bite-sized mantras that reflect the behaviours necessary to bring your vision to life. And once you have these ready to go, it's time for the next challenge – to bring your vision to the world.

MANTRA
/ˈmantrə/

NOUN

1. (ORIGINALLY IN HINDUISM AND BUDDHISM) A WORD OR SOUND REPEATED TO AID CONCENTRATION IN MEDITATION.
2. A STATEMENT OR SLOGAN REPEATED FREQUENTLY.

GOLDEN NUGGETS
ENVISION

Game-changing leaders are dreamers.
Start by dreaming big!

Focus on purpose, start with 'why.'

Craft a vision that touches the hearts and minds of
every member of the team.

Ask the strategic question: "What are we missing?"
Identify the opportunity.

Treat the vision-crafting process like a treasure.
Make time for it.

Listen carefully, the answers are in the room.

Imagine a world where your vision is reality.
How does it feel? What does it look like?

There is no 'one-size-fits-all' formula for envisioning.
Create your process and trust it.

CHAPTER 4

EXPRESS

Express with a focus on creating
a burning sense of dissatisfaction
with the status quo.

Congratulations! You've taken the first big step in crafting your vision, making it compelling and personal. As we discovered together, it's not easy to create such a vision that captures the logic of the 'what' and the emotion of the 'why.' Creating the vision and giving it a tangible shape is the first important step toward changing the game as a leader.

The next challenge is to **express** it – to take this thoughtful, well-crafted vision out the door and share it with the world. And to do it in the hope that the team will feel just as passionately as you do as its architect. In order to bring your vision to life, to push the buttons, and to inspire to action, it must be shared in an impactful way. This can happen only if you communicate the vision in a way that *matters*.

"Sometimes life hits you in the head with a brick. Don't lose faith. I'm convinced that the only thing that kept me going was that I loved what I did. You've got to find what you love."
Steve Jobs, Stanford University, 2005

"No matter what challenges or setbacks or disappointments you may encounter along the way, you will find true success and happiness if you have only one goal, there really is only one, and that is this: to fulfil the highest most truthful expression of yourself as a human being."
Oprah Winfrey, Harvard University, 2013

" ... I learned, every youth wants to be unique, that is, YOU! But the world around you is doing its best day and night to make you just like everybody else. Now the question is whether you want to be YOU or everybody else. Being like everybody else is convenient at first glance, but not satisfying in long vision.

" ... There are four things you need to have to win that battle. The first is to set the goal, the second is to acquire knowledge continuously, the third is work hard with devotion and the fourth is perseverance. If you have these four tools, then you will definitely become UNIQUE YOU ... "
Abdul J Kalam, IIT, Chennai, India, 2010

"My father could have been a great comedian, but he didn't believe that that was possible for him. And so he made a conservative choice. Instead, he got a safe job as an account-ant, and when I was 12 years old, he was let go from that safe job, and our family had to do whatever we could to survive. I learned many great lessons from my father. Not the least of which was that you can fail at what you don't want, so you might as well take a chance on doing what you love."
Jim Carrey, Maharashi University of Management, 2014

"I was set free, because my greatest fear had been realized, and I was still alive, and I still had a daughter whom I adored, and I had an old typewriter and a big idea."
JK Rowling, Harvard University, 2008

Excerpts from speeches of five inspiring personalities. What do these speeches have in common? They are authentic, from the heart. And each one has the magical expression of a compelling vision.

Steve Jobs' shared three stories that gave a riveting perspective on loss, recovery and finding a job you love. Oprah Winfrey's words powerfully expressed the strength of resilience. And JK Rowling brought out its hope and belief. Abdul Kalam had the students engaged and inspired on a topic that confident youngsters don't much prefer to hear from adults. Jim Carrey's used his own magical talent of comedy and drama to express the inevitability of failure, and that it's okay to fail. And he did it in a most positive manner.

The reflections and suggestions came from the personal journeys of these speakers. Their words were authentic, showing a sense of vulnerability that is rarely seen among celebrities. In turn, it ignited a sense of purpose, hope and pride in the young graduates.

The game-changing leader takes a vision and makes it real. The leader takes the team on a journey, touching their minds and hearts, and igniting a fire that encourages the team to believe. And when the team *believes*, the vision begins to take on a life of its own – and the passion for it becomes contagious. At that point, the game-changing leader simply steps aside and lets the movement unfold.

And so here we are at the next E – **express**.

Express is more than just informing or communicating the vision. It's about bringing it to life through a message, through storytelling and walking the talk. It's about delivering a compelling message that is personal, logical, emotional, passionate and consistent at every touchpoint.

Let's assume that you've hit the jackpot in creating the right vision for the right moment. It's sharp. It's succinct. It pushes the right buttons. And better yet, you have included the team in your efforts to bring the vision alive. What is so clear in your head is now on paper and ready to be shared. How do you bring this carefully crafted vision to your universe? Your world may be a small team or a complex organization that spans many demographics, cultures and borders. This is your moment of truth to express the vision in a way that touches everyone. Get it right and the possibilities to lay the seeds of an amazing movement are endless. Get it wrong and the vision crumbles. Unfortunately, it's at the **express** stage where many leaders drop the ball.

It's helpful to look at some of the common denominators that make people tick when it comes to followership. A vision that unleashes the 'spirit of one' is a powerful start. The sense that we are all in this together, regardless of the role in the organization, level, job title or tenure. It's true that there is no 'I' in team, but there is an 'I' in ignite, inspire, impact and win, and there are two in vision. This 'I' stands for a unified team that stands together in spirit and in its shared mission and values.

Before we dive into 'how' game-changing leaders express their vision successfully, let's look at some reasons others don't. It begins with being connected with the frontline, the audience that the leader intends to influence. How can a leader touch the members of the team if they don't understand their challenges, joys, pain and ambitions?

So, while the vision may make good sense and may be what the organization really needs, the team will not respond or react to the vision if they can't connect with it. Perhaps it's simply too logical.

It's interesting to observe that the exceptional leaders among us are the ones who have a solid balance between logic and emotion. The leader who leans toward logic, supported by data, tends to be out of touch. These leaders use language that is not the language of the team. The leader talks about a vision in theoretical terms and focused on measurable outcomes. Important, yes, but not aligned with the individual goals of the team members. To make matters worse, these leaders ignore the motivators for their teams and talk about a future that is important for themselves but irrelevant to the team. And the reaction, or lack of a reaction, frustrates these leaders.

Such leaders typically say things like:
- "It's not my fault that they don't get it …"
- "No matter how many times I repeat the message they just don't get it … maybe I need to dumb it down …"
- "I'm tired of repeating the same message over and over again …"
- "I've done my part, now it's up to the team to get it done …"

And why does this happen? Interestingly, more often than not, the problem isn't with the vision itself, it's about 'how' the leader expresses the vision.

"MAN OFTEN BECOMES
WHAT HE BELIEVES
HIMSELF TO BE."

MAHATMA GANDHI

Steve Jobs is often cited as an example of a leader who 'expressed' his vision in a magical way to inspire action. But what many don't notice is how he used language and the powerful pause to deliver his message for impact. Let's take a closer look at an excerpt from his speech on the launch of the iPod, a game-changing innovation.[8]

"The coolest thing about iPod is that your entire music library fits in your pocket. OK? You can take your whole music library with you, right in your pocket. Never before possible. So that's iPod."

Now, read the quote from Steve Jobs one more time, and this time, *be Steve Jobs*. Express the words with passion, with volume, with emphasis, use the powerful pause and deliver the knockout punch, **"Never before possible."** Even better if you say it out loud, with impact; just make sure nobody is peeking over your shoulder!

Here we go …

"The coolest thing about iPod is that your **entire** music library fits in your pocket …

OK?

You can take your **whole** music library with you, right in your pocket!

Never. Before. Possible.

So **that's** iPod."

Drop the mic! Small tweaks in the delivery, with passion and pause, takes a strong statement and makes it a bold, powerful expression of an already ambitious vision.

FIND YOUR **TRUE NORTH**

Earlier in the chapter on **envision**, I talked about my own experience in taking the lead of an underperforming organization. The compass survey was conducted, which then led to the 'compass offsite' of the leaders of the organization. First, I needed to understand what the perception of the organization's direction was, including the common points, the overlaps. These would become the levers for change. At the same time, I needed to understand the gaps, uncommon goals, and the anomalies that divided the team.

The compass offsite is a chance to reflect on the responses from the survey and make conclusions. From this, you can co-create mantras, your guiding principles that will eventually form the base of your North Star. This is the moment for the leadership team to make some bold decisions on the future direction. In the case of the organization I was leading, we discovered that we had fallen into the trap of going wide and shallow, doing a lot but accomplishing very little. So, we adopted these principles: to do more from less. To be specialists rather than generalists.

We also accepted the fact that we had become an organization too focused on the legacy and were looking back and using language like, "That's the way we've always done it," and "We've already tried that, it didn't work." So, we embraced a future-focused mantra:

to honour the past but focus on the future. And there was clearly a silo culture with the toxic habit of pointing fingers at others when things didn't go as planned. Perhaps these principles were the most difficult to introduce and bring to life in the organization. To look in the mirror, and to raise the bar. And to behave as one team, in the spirit of one unified team, heading collectively in the same direction and united, as we worked together to achieve our goals.

And then began the fun part of expressing this exciting vision to the organization. In giving expression to the vision we crafted, we went bold. We knew we were not in the leading position in our industry. Nor were we the most admired company. Far from it. So, we set out to achieve both, and expressed it in our vision. This bold ambition captured the minds and hearts of our people. It became a rallying call, a collaborative endeavour. You could call it our own version of a BHAG (big, hairy, audacious goal). Or, as Salim Ismail says in the book *Exponential Organizations*,[9] the compelling vision should be taken one step further as a MTP (massive transformative purpose). This is a purpose that is not about maintaining the status quo or playing the game better, but more focused on changing the game.

So, game-changing leadership begins with having a game-changing purpose. Let's repeat this message that all great leaders know well. Business outcomes are exactly that – outcomes. The financial result is the proof of concept; better yet, it's proof of the vision. Bring the right people together, with a compelling vision and the tools required to bring the vision to life, and the chance of success is high.

The **express** piece is a very sensitive and critical aspect of leadership, whether you're communicating your vision or simply sharing an update on progress. The same rules apply as we learned at the **envision** stage. Impactful expression calls for cocreation. In the spirit of 'two ears one mouth,' begin by asking questions. And more importantly, make sure you listen to the answers. There are no shortcuts when it comes to giving your team members a voice. Leaders who take the time to listen and gather the voice of their people first have a much greater chance of expressing their vision with impact. And the first rule in communicating effectively is to connect with the audience. It's absolutely critical that you communicate your vision in a way that touches the entire audience and not just a single demographic or selective segments of the audience. When you consider how much thought and effort have been put into your vision, it would be a shame if it doesn't touch the majority of the team, the very people responsible for driving it.

Let me briefly step back to my 'pre-envision' days, when I was a brand-new leader in the Indian arm of my organization. This is the time when the new leader needs to gather the ingredients that will come together to form the foundation of the vision. I spent the first two months on a mission to listen. And so, as I said earlier, I criss-crossed the corners of the organization and the country to get a first-hand look at the pulse of the team I was commissioned to lead.

It was a marvellous eye-opener. I had an in-depth understanding of their ambitions and their challenges. I revelled in their pride and joy of belonging to the organization and empathized equally with the barriers and their frustrations in realizing their ambitions. The more I listened to them, the more I discovered strong patterns of similarities and overlaps in their motivational buttons. I made notes from our conversations and, in the process, created a word bank of the most commonly used words and phrases. This would prove to be very helpful as I began to express my vision in the weeks and months that followed.

So, first get out there, spend time with your team. Use your two ears to listen – and one mouth to ask those probing questions. Get to the core, find the buttons … and then get prepared to push those buttons again and again.

Effective expression of your vision is not about using awe-inspiring technical terminology or theoretical jargon. Jargon is defined by the *Cambridge Dictionary* as "language used by a particular group of people, especially in their work, and which most other people do not understand." If your objective is not to confuse your audience, keep the message simple and in a language that is clear and laser sharp. Leave no doubt.

Think about your favourite teacher back in your school days, the one who took something very complicated and somehow made it easy to understand. This is an important skill, which every leader must develop. By keeping your message simple, digestible and memorable, you'll connect with your audience and, in turn, start to build followership.

This is the power of the language in expression. The right language is a powerful tool for game-changing leaders. On the other hand, using the wrong language is a sure way to alienate your team and sabotage your message. Creating a cloud of the most commonly used words and phrases unveils patterns that are invaluable to expressing ourselves. And it helps give you focus as you work toward the next phase of the E5.

The beauty of identifying patterns early on is that it gives leaders a head start in making the 'right language' choices to reach out to different segments of their audience. Repetitive patterns make it easier to fix communication for things that are not going so right. For things that are working well, it helps to drive acceleration in doing them even better. Weaving the right patterns to the right people at the right time can have a huge impact.

Some of the old adage practices of 'speaking the same language' are timeless. Paraphrasing, for one, is a great way of building a connection. Familiar language breeds a sense of inclusion, that the leader is 'one of us,' and is 'in the game.' To take it one step further, the leader who asks probing questions, using the language of the team, and in the right tone that shows interest – that leader has found an extremely positive tool for engaging their audience.

The right language can also be nonverbal. Meeting the eye, imperceptible nods of understanding, smiles of encouragement, or leaning forward to show that they have your full attention – are equally important when listening and while expressing.

It takes diligent effort and a genuine desire to connect to achieve this end. People are quick to switch off from the leader who does not speak their language. And then there is no point in a leader's frustrated lament of, "No matter how many times I say it, they just don't get it."

I'm a big believer in the power of language to create a culture, set the tone, and to lay the foundation of a movement. The game-changing leader is very aware of the power of language when expressing the vision. Leaders must choose their words carefully but be careful not to sound rehearsed. You are most impactful when you're authentic. My goal is to be a leader who is authentic, who delivers the message without a filter, sometimes tough and at other times not. From both the heart and mind, and always with the objective to inspire my teams to action. To be better than yesterday – this is the art of effective messaging.

There is some science in how inspirational leaders deliver their message. We know that an amazing neuro lingual process occurs when we speak. In fact, there is a lightning-speed process happening when a leader delivers a message. It begins with the thought, the instantaneous planning, which happens in the brain. This then triggers the mouth to change shape, and the vocal chords to deliver sounds with tones, enunciation and tempo. And for those of us who follow our parents' age-old advice, 'think before you speak,' we even imagine the potential or, better yet, the intended reaction of our words from the listener(s). All of this happens faster than the blink of an eye. So, to choose the right words with the right tone, speed and posture takes practice. Language triggers certain reactions. Becoming acutely self-aware and sensitive to the words we use to express our vision, and the reactions they generate, is an important step toward becoming a reflective leader.

Here's a great lesson in how to express a compelling message. To express something that is powerful, it's very important to tap back into the word cloud that you've created and do three things. First, identify things that have gone well. At the same time, your vision should also address what is not going well – but do so in a manner of challenging the status quo in a positive way. Second, tie the expression of your vision to optimism. Encourage the team to dream. Ask the important questions: "Let's see how we can do this …" and "What if we …?" Third, take the words directly from the word cloud and build the language of the team into your vision.

Let's assume that you've reached out to your team. You've spent time with them. You've asked questions and paid attention to what they have to say. You've probed, discussed and gathered feedback, collecting your notes and observations. This is a good time to turn inward, a time to reflect and ask yourself, "What did I learn from the interaction?" "What are the patterns?" "Which stories will be featured in my message when I stand in front of my teams?" These stories, the real examples, will play a crucial role in expressing your vision in an authentic and impactful way.

Game-changing leaders take advantage of the moment, especially when it comes to expressing their vision to the world. The message can be a bit nostalgic, while also talking about the future. It's important to strike a balance. 'Honour the past' means sharing respect for the past and the contributions of those who helped bring us from there to here. 'Focus on the future' means sharing the excitement of what we can accomplish together. 'Stand on the shoulders of giants' means expressing our willingness to collaborate and envision the path to success. Ultimately, the future-focused leader expresses a crystal-clear message that we will drive the good stuff and fix – or better yet remove – the bad stuff.

TIPS: EXPRESS YOUR VISION TO ENGAGE AND INSPIRE

Become a storyteller.
Bring your vision alive by telling real stories. Capture the hearts and minds by being authentic.

Make your abbreviated 'elevator speech' equally exciting.
You will have to talk about it in the elevator, at the car park, over a quick cup of coffee and as you briefly greet your people. Keep the energy pumping in short bursts too.

Keep the message omnipresent.
Embrace omnichannel communication. Identify the touchpoints and create a strategy to trigger them. Express the message repeatedly and consistently from a variety of angles.

The importance of communicating the vision through different media cannot be overstressed. Especially in today's digital world, where the younger generation – the up-and-coming work-force – has literally grown up with mobiles and tablets in their hands. This is the generation that communicates in 140 characters through Twitter, Instagram and Snapchat. We need to communicate with them the same way they communicate with one another.

But we also have another generation – an older one – that needs to be addressed. Unlike Millennials, the 'perennials,' as I affectionately call them, grew up in a world of expression. They explain context in full sentences, they meet people face to face, and use that old-fashioned communication machine called the telephone. This generation moved through well-planned stages to reach a conclusion. The **express** strategy needs to include them with the same commitment. In essence, the message has to be expressed in a manner that is appealing to everyone in the organization.

In the world of marketing, omnichannel transforms the experience of a product and brand with every customer interaction. In expressing a vision or message, it should do no less. Our people are the customers who will be placed at the centre. Our approach to them must be aligned to their actions, both online and offline.

Town halls, vlogs, blogs, posts on social media and the old-fashioned internal newsletter – all are effective vehicles to share your message. If the 'why' was the hero in **envision**, the 'how' becomes the star in **express**.

What does this mean for you as a leader? You have to be genuine at all times and be consistent in your message across every channel you choose. The same passion, the same message, the same vision. And you can achieve this only when you constantly revisit your vision, and the North Star you've created for the team. It's crucial to keep the message aligned and true.

Add a personal touch.
Leverage technology for touch, but don't ignore the power of sharing your vision face to face. Keep your message human, make it real through real stories.

Find the button.
Research shows that most shoppers don't click the 'buy' button on Amazon on their first visit.[10] That magical click – the commitment to hand over hard-earned money – comes after multiple touchpoints. Let's trace this journey.

The potential buyer may look at the item once, say on his tablet, in the morning. He most probably will go to other websites for more research. How does the same product compare on multiple sites? Or, how do other products compare with it? The information floats in his mind – and perhaps he comes back to it again a few hours later on his laptop or desktop – maybe for some more data. He may look at it again on the way home – this time on his mobile, perhaps – all the while gathering more information from friends and other reviews. At leisure, say after dinner, he may go to the app and click the order button.

Expressing the vision to push the 'accept' button with people is a very similar experience. As leaders, there are two very important takeaways from the Amazon example. The first is that one touchpoint isn't enough. Like shoppers, the buy-in of the vision does not happen the first time. Or even the second or third. The rule goes as follows: 'Repeat, repeat, repeat and repeat.' The statistics vary but general consensus among marketing professionals says that you need to touch the consumer five to seven times before they will commit to buy. These touchpoints lead to the moment of truth, the purchase, which in the case of a leader expressing the vision is translated as digesting, embracing and leaning in.

Mix it up.
We need to adopt a multifaceted and omnichannel marketing strategy. Typically what happens is that the vision is created, crafted and drafted, most probably with the support of the marketing team. And then it's brought to the floor where the leader will express it in speeches, emails, town halls and focus groups. Simultaneously, the message will go up on the walls and signs dangling from the ceiling. These are good first steps. However, when we look at the omnichannel approach to expressing the vision, it needs to be executed in a holistic manner.

Mike Babcock, coach of the Toronto Maple Leafs in the National Hockey League is one of the 'winningest' ice hockey coaches in the world. He's the only coach to be in the Triple Gold Club, guiding the Detroit Red Wings to the coveted Stanley Cup in 2008, leading Team Canada to gold medal wins at the IIHF Ice Hockey World Championship in 2004, the 2010 Olympics

TRANSFORMATIVE LEADERS CONFRONT THE BRUTAL FACTS. THEY CHOOSE TO PURSUE *BETTER*. AND THEY LEAVE NO DOUBT.

in Vancouver and again in 2014 in Sochi. He also coached the IIHF World Junior Championship team in 1997 and led the turnaround of the University of Lethbridge hockey program, bringing the team to win the CIS University Cup in 1994. Clearly, this coach knows how to build winning teams!

It's no surprise that Coach Babcock is a passionate student of leadership. In his book, *Leave No Doubt: A Credo for Chasing Your Dreams*,[11] he talks about the importance of the role of the leader to set the tone in the room, to build a sense of belief in the vision, and to *"own the pressure"* that the bold and ambitious goal brings. The role of the game-changing leader is to make the critical moments *happen*. His coaching philosophy is his leadership philosophy, and it's rooted in three simple but powerful words: **leave no doubt**.

This mantra hangs on the walls of the locker rooms where he has coached. It's a powerful message for all leaders – when you express your vision, do it with full and utter conviction. He left no doubt.

The game-changing leader is fiercely committed to achieving the goal. These leaders don't mix words, they are unequivocal in defining the '*what*,' '*why*' and the '*how*.' The '*who*' and '*when*' are important pieces of the puzzle that follow naturally. Such leaders search for the balance between being visionary, operating at a macro-level while also being pragmatic and down in the mud with the team. In every single encounter, whether a town hall, team meeting, through marketing channels or one-to-one over coffee, they deliver the same, consistent message.

And with each opportunity to express and share the vision with the team, they *leave no doubt*.

Review, seek out feedback and revise.
A great way to avoid mediocrity is to be self-critical. Have the confidence and humility to invite feedback and advice. And ask yourself and a trusted peer some hard questions:
- How was my message delivered?
- How was my message received?
- Did we accomplish the goal of communicating the message effectively?
- Did it push our people's buttons? How do we know for sure?
- Will it inspire them to action?
- What did we miss?

Of course, we run the risk of getting answers that are not what we want to hear. And many leaders have an issue with this. Ego takes over, and they make the classic mistake of becoming defensive. But your team wants a reason to believe before they jump on board and are ready to take action.

Communicate, communicate ... and communicate again for good measure.
This is the golden rule for express. There's simply no such thing as overcommunication when it comes to expressing your vision. Communication needs to be dynamic and fluid in a way that is unique to you and catered to your team. And with each touchpoint, the message needs to be consistent and authentic.

YOU'RE NOT JUST
SHARING YOUR VISION.
YOU'RE TELLING THE
STORY OF YOUR VISION.

THE IMPACTFUL
LEADER, THEN,
IS A STORYTELLER.

Leaders are, in a sense, teachers. And the best teachers understand their learners. You're not just sharing your vision; you are *teaching* it. When you take on the role of a teacher, understanding how your team members learn becomes crucial for success. How effectively you express your vision, then, has a direct impact as you move to the next phase.

And this is where the wheels of change start to move.

GOLDEN NUGGETS
EXPRESS

Express is about bringing the vision to life.

Do a pulse check before you express your vision
and know your audience.

Be a storyteller, make it real, make it fun. Make it human.

Imagine what the world looks like when your vision
becomes reality. Share it with anyone who will listen.

Use the pause ...

Measure success through your audience.
Make them sit up, lean in and want more.

Success is where preparation and opportunity meet.
Practise your message, ask for feedback
and practise it again.

Before you get on the stage, focus on the end objective
– to inspire the team to action.

CHAPTER 5

EXCITE

In order to excite, the leader needs
to connect. And excitement comes
from being connected.

The 1980 Winter Olympics has gone down in history as perhaps one of the best examples of good athletes achieving greatness. The 'Miracle on Ice,' as it came to be known, is an iconic story of a team with a visionary coach as their leader, supported by a very solid strategy, a deep sense of belief and passion and, ultimately, execution of the plan by the team. It stands as a great testimony of how inspiring leadership can ignite a spark, which leads to greatness.

On the face of it, the ice hockey pool in 1980 was a lopsided competition. The Soviet Union had won the gold medal in five of the six previous Winter Olympic Games and was the clear favourite to win once more in Lake Placid, New York. The Russian team was filled with professional players from the KHL and top European leagues. These players came with deep experience in international play. The top players from the USA, on the other hand, played in the NHL, arguably the best professional league in the world. However, the NHL would not allow its players to compete in the Olympics. And so, Team USA was an exclusive collection of amateurs, largely college-level players. With an average age of 22 years, they were the youngest team in the Olympic tournament and the youngest in US national team history.

Most people assumed the team would be knocked out of the competition in the early rounds and wouldn't be able to keep up with the highly talented Russians, Finns and Czechs. As Team USA would soon prove to the world, one should never doubt the power of a vision and what can happen when a team *believes*.

CHAPTER 5 – EXCITE

Just before the semi-final game against the Russians, the coach of Team USA, Herb Brooks, stood in front of his mishmash of young, relatively mediocre players and gave this speech.

"Great moments are born from great opportunity, and that's what you have here tonight, boys," he exhorted. "That's what you've earned here tonight. One game. If we played them ten times, they might win nine. But not this game, not tonight. Tonight, we skate with them. Tonight we stay with them, and we shut them down because we can.

Tonight, we are the greatest hockey team in the world. You were born to be hockey players—every one of you, and you were meant to be here tonight …

Screw 'em. This is *your* time. Now go out there and take it!"[12]

Herb Brooks had a vision before the tournament even started. He put a long list of prospects through gruelling on-ice tryouts combined with equally demanding psychometric tests, to gain a deeper understanding of each player's emotions, response under stress, commitment and passion to win.

In other words, the players sitting in front of him just minutes before facing off against the Russian elite squad had been hand-picked, not solely for their technical hockey skills, but also for their character. He knew the motivational buttons of every single player on the team, and Brooks was famous for pushing those buttons relentlessly until he got the response he was looking for.

EXCITE BEGINS WHEN THE LEADER BELIEVES ...

So, when he delivered this speech, he knew exactly what needed to be said. He nailed the critical E, **excite**, which would inspire action. This was the moment of truth.

The starting point of creating a compelling vision is to envision; the vision is something that is imagined. It doesn't become real until it's expressed. Do you get to see the inspiration? Do you create an exciting sense of "Let's do this"? Herb Brooks' stirring speech, which was followed by a legendary performance was, in fact, scribbled out on a piece of paper, but the passion and emotions it ignited in the young men were incredible. Before a frenzied crowd of 10,000 spectators, and millions around the world watching on TV, they defeated the Soviet team 4–3. And two days later, they further shocked the world when they clinched the gold for their country, beating the highly favoured Finnish team, 4–2.

There is a direct connection with what Coach Brooks faced and what we encounter in our own leadership challenges. Think of those times when you were preparing to stand in front of your team, to share your vision, with the aim to crystallize the future and inspire the team to action. This is the power of **excite**. We'll dig into this critical element of inspirational leadership in this chapter.

But first, let's look at your journey so far with the E5:
- As an engaged leader, you've listened to your people.
- You've taken care to understand what strums their motivational strings.
- You've created a compelling vision born out of close interaction with your leaders and employees.

- And you've strategized how you will communicate the vision to make it real. To make it bold. To fire their imagination and make it matter to your employees. To take the most effective omnichannel route to reach out and deliver it as an experience.

And now, as you bring this carefully crafted message to the floor, how can you be sure that the message has hit the 'sweet spot' of engagement? Are they really 'leaning in'? By the time you've finished your presentation, is your team ready to jump out of their seats and get at it? Or are they slowly making their way back to their workstations, defaulting to their usual routine?

Leadership requires the ability to influence. The ability to influence ignites action, it inspires people to stand up and move with energy and focus. Influence then, is about creating a sense of excitement. Now, measuring 'excitement' is a tough thing to do. You can use engagement surveys or simply *ask* employees how they feel about the vision that was expressed. What attracted them to the vision? What made them feel excited about it? And equally important, what was missing?

It can be risky for some leaders to ask their employees if the vision touches them, because it requires an openness to the possibility that team members aren't touched by your vision. And this can hurt, especially after how hard you worked on crafting it in the first place. This is an important lesson of leadership – the need for humility. We've all been humbled at some time in our leadership journey, and it's in those moments of reflection that we have an opportunity to grow and improve on our quest to be game-changing leaders.

It's a common assumption to believe that employees will just 'get it.' The trouble with this assumption, however, is that it balloons into a denial-driven belief that asserts, "If they don't get it, it's all their fault, their problem."

The process of calibrating, of measuring and verifying that the message that was intended to be delivered is actually being received and digested is very important. If not, the leader risks falling in the trap of 'Chinese Whispers.' That is, as the message is delivered by the leader, it's then passed along to others in team meetings, chats by the coffee machine and in text messages. Over time, and as it passes hands, the message can be diluted, reversed and modified to the point where it's unrecognizable. The misinterpretation that can follow can have a negative impact on the efforts to bring the original vision to life.

Let's be optimistic for a moment. Let's assume you have a well-crafted vision that touches the hearts and minds of the team. You're absolutely confident that your vision is solid, meaningful, aspirational and connects with the desires and motivations of the team. You've crafted an omnichannel approach to expressing your vision. And you're ready to hit the road.

In many ways, this is the moment of truth. How can you ensure that you'll kick-start the excitement that you're aiming to generate as you express your vision? Stay on point, keep it laser sharp. Honour and protect the message, which you've worked so hard to create. I cannot emphasize this point enough. Be consistent in delivering your message, firmly rooted in the vision.

Every year in November and December, I go on a roadshow, visiting the four corners of the organization I lead. In my current role, that means 25 offices across India. I deliver our two-year plan under the theme 'Our Vision.' And rooted in this is always the vision, the 'North Star,' the 'True North,' or whatever you want to call it. I celebrate with them what has brought us from there to here. We honour the past and focus on the future. And together, we look ahead with optimism at what the future will look like when we bring the vision to reality.

Of course, we adjust as we go. But we don't zigzag on the message. We may pivot, depending on the circumstances, but we stay consistent. And I constantly remind myself about this important point. If I can excite my teams across locations, from the front end to the middle and to the very back end of my organization – we are almost certain to reach our goal.

But in order to do so, my message needs to be consistent. I must bring the same level of passion, clarity and energy to every individual or group I meet with. And then I need to recalibrate, reconfirm, and make sure that I did, in fact, deliver my message in a powerfully compelling way. So, be consistent. Deliver the same presentation with the same level of commitment and passion every time. Be authentic, not rehearsed. Get feedback, calibrate, pulse check, recalibrate and do it again.

As leaders, we've all experienced those moments of frustration, those times that in spite of the effort to share the message, people 'just don't get it.' You wonder, "Why is my audience not responding?" Or the more revealing one that says, "Where's the energy? What's wrong with them?"

Many leaders who I speak to are especially discouraged by the feeling of frustration in the lack of response to their call to action (what I call the 'leader lament'). And the blame game inevitably follows. It's no surprise that these leaders typically show a lack of self-awareness. Instead of looking in the mirror, they tend to default to pointing fingers.

I remember the time when, over dinner, the CEO of a large multinational company shared his experience of how he conveys his messages to his people. This CEO had taken over from his predecessor who was quite charismatic. Not necessarily a visionary, but one of those leaders who commanded the stage and who could rock his audience. But this leader was quite the opposite. He was stoic and monotonic in delivering his message. He firmly believed that to excite was not really the key role of a leader.

He would stand in front of the gathering and say, "Let me just make it clear. If you expect me to inspire you, well don't. That's not the kind of leader I am. But what I will do is show you the way to success." You cannot fault this CEO for the clarity of his message. He let his people know, loud and clear, that he was not the one to inspire them, but that it was up to them to inspire themselves. Full marks for honesty, would you say? Perhaps … but I have some misgivings about that.

If you begin the conversation with a bold comment about what you *won't* do as a leader, then you can expect that you will immediately alienate a segment of the audience. The fact is, some people expect – no, need – their leader to inspire and excite them. If you stand with confidence and conviction and state, "I'm not here to excite you," you can expect a reaction that matches the intention. Rest assured that people will NOT be excited!

Inspiration may come in many different ways. But excitement is where the magic happens. It's the moment of inspiration to action and when the movement begins. It may not be about what's said, but it's certainly about how it's said. And as many masters of the microphone know well, inspiration can come even from the silence between words. The pregnant pause.

Back in 1876, many of Thomas Edison's band of men – called the 'Muckers' – worked with Edison for their entire lives. Often, when they came to him, they were fresh out of college or technical training. The average work week was six days and a total of 55 hours. And if Edison had a bright idea, workdays would become work nights too.

Edison was not known for his charisma. In fact, one mucker has said that Edison "Could wither one with his biting sarcasm or ridicule one into extinction." Yet, his electrician, Arthur Kennelly, has stated, "The privilege which I had being with this great man for six years was the greatest inspiration of my life."[13]

So, what made Edison's Muckers excited? Somewhere, somehow, Edison consistently pushed their buttons to see the bigger purpose of their ambition to work. Maybe it was his vision with which he created the first industrial research laboratory in Menlo Park, New Jersey. Maybe it was the passion that the 'Wizard of Menlo Park' (as Edison was called) ignited in his invention factory among his team of inventors – who saw a bunch of their inventions touch the lives of people. Fast forward to Steve Jobs. When he returned to Apple in 1997 as CEO, he began building his own version of Edison's Muckers in the secret rooms of the research and development department.

Edison and Jobs teach us an important lesson. They both knew that charisma was not enough to inspire greatness. Instead, they discovered at some point that people are inspired by dreams. And so, they shared their dreams, as bizarre and far-fetched as they may have sounded. It's little wonder that historians believe that Edison's greatest invention was, in fact, his research and development laboratory. For Jobs, he was most comfortable tinkering away on his top-secret projects with his Mac engineers, and on retreats telling his teams that the work they were doing was going to send a giant ripple through the universe.

Inspiration to excite can come in many forms. The expression of the vision doesn't have to be loud with lots of fist pumping and rah-rah, but it needs a pitch; the kind of tone that pierces the mind and heart. If your aim is to generate a sense of excitement about your vision (and it should be!), it's important to push these buttons:

- Convey the greater purpose with crystal-clear clarity
- Paint a picture of what the world will look like when the vision is brought to life
- Enthuse people with an authentic 'what's in it for them'

If you miss these key triggers at the **excite** phase, the momentum of the E5 slows to a crawl. I've seen it happen often with some of the CEOs who come to me for advice. They've crafted a powerful and well-thought-out vision, put in place a solid strategy to get it out there and then went out to the world to share their message. And in many cases, they use a clever omnichannel approach to deliver it. But they simply were not able to excite their people nor inspire them to action. A pity, because this stage is pivotal.

Why is this? In most cases, these leaders simply missed the key buttons mentioned above. Instead, these leaders fell into the jargon trap, focusing more on the aesthetics of their message rather than the purpose and impact. The old adage 'keep it simple' is at the core of **excite** and inspires teams to action.

IGNITE **CURIOSITY**

There are some great examples of leaders over history who have displayed an amazing ability to find and push the right buttons. Martin Luther King, Jr was certainly one. His four words, "I have a dream … " with that loaded pause was an electrifying moment.

You see, when someone says, "I have a dream," the looming question in the minds of a large majority of listeners is, "What is it?" Martin Luther King, Jr pressed this curiosity button in the opening words of his historic address, and he immediately had the entire audience leaning in.

Curiosity is immensely powerful. As a game-changing leader, when you can ignite this curiosity early on in your message, people will sit up, and a sense of anticipation builds. This engagement and the connection with the audience is the first important step to building excitement. You also need to unravel the message in a way that attracts the majority of the audience. Remember, the aim is to ignite the fire, to create a movement.

Reverend King did this in a masterful way. He went on to express a dream that was not just relevant to a certain member or demographic, but to every single person at the gathering. He used a language that had more of the 'we,' the 'us' and the 'as one,' regardless of colour and political affiliations. It did not matter where they sat on the psychometric paradigm, as everyone could relate to what he was saying – a world without prejudice or bias, a world where everyone had equal opportunities, a world of peace. He had found the common button.

Martin Luther King, Jr delivered his message in a masterful way, using the mechanics of 'voice and volume.' And if you listen carefully, he used the pregnant pause for astounding impact. I encourage all leaders who aspire to be game changers, who wish to be impactful in expressing their vision, to watch video clips of leaders who excelled in this ability.

Again, back to Steve Jobs, another classic example of the power of delivery to ignite change. What most people don't know is that he wasn't naturally good on stage. In fact, he didn't like being on stage. But Steve Jobs had a flair for drama. And he was convinced that, as CEO of Apple, he was commissioned with this role of being the salesman of the entrepreneurial vision of the company and his bold dreams for the future.

Jobs understood that, in order to create a movement, he needed to get on the stage and wave the flag and create a sense of suspense in the process. His messages were less about the product and more about how the people in the room had an opportunity to use the product as the vehicle to change the world.

So how did he do it? Like King, Jobs used the element of voice very effectively. His voice had a unique high-pitched tone and, let's face it, there's something that can be both exciting and annoying about a high-pitched voice. The same is true with a low-pitched voice, the monotone that inevitably leads many to take a nap during a well-intentioned speech.

Whether or not he liked being on stage, Steve Jobs leveraged his flair for drama. He was able to use his high-pitched voice in a way that contrasted and counterbalanced his low-pitched tones. And if you hear the way he used his vowels, you can tell that clearly, he had some coaching, or at least he gave it plenty of thought. His presentation was always spot on when it came to using the pitch, pause and timing.

Excitement is also about engaging with the audience. There is a school of thought in presentations that says we should not be asking questions. We should be giving answers. But I don't necessarily believe that. We should provoke and prompt thought when we are engaging with our audience.

In my own reviews and in my presentations, I ask a lot of questions. I focus on eliciting thoughts and feedback. And I prompt the audience to think. This is not just with individuals or smaller groups. It's equally important to ask probing, open-ended questions with larger groups. By pushing the buttons of the seeking mind, you start a conversation. Conversations then lead to new ideas. And, as all game-changing leaders know well, ideas are the seeds of transformation.

In your meetings with your teams, try to create a dialogue. As a leader, you may be interacting with 500 people – or even more. But to the individual in the audience, it must feel like a conversation, a one-on-one interaction. Not an easy task, but so powerful when you get it right. Another reason to reach out to the experts for help – it's no surprise that presidents and prime ministers have speech writers.

With some effort and practise, you can develop this skill. It begins with asking the right questions, the ones that prompt people to think and to dream. My favourite question to ask one-on-one or in a large audience is, "What if … ?" You'll see the reaction immediately: eyes start to gaze upwards as the seeking mind is activated.

Or, call out the sales folk in the gathering and address them: "All the salespeople in the room raise your hands. What if you, as salespeople, started doing this one thing differently?" And you explain what that one thing is that can be done differently and have them tell you what the impact would be.

Pause for a minute here and consider. What have you done with these simple questions? You've created a dialogue. You're engaging in a conversation with your team and sending out a clear message that you're ready to co-create the answers.

Let's flip the pages of history. In 1994, Nelson Mandela was elected as the first black president of South Africa, four years after he was released from a 27-year incarceration. As epochal as it was, newly elected Mandela was aware that his nation still remained racially and economically divided in the wake of apartheid. His passion to end this impasse created a powerful vision of bringing his people together through sport.

It was a hugely wild dream to have rugby as the unifying sport – a sport that was the love of the whites and totally despised by blacks, who looked at it as the symbol of a racist rule. As charismatic as he was, and as powerful as his vision was, and despite the awe and authority he wielded, Mandela had the humility to know that a unified South Africa needed to be built together.

His partner? Francois Pienaar, captain of the Springboks team. Between them, they ploughed through the initial period of doubt and scepticism, creating sparks of excitement as the players interacted with fans to form friendships. By the second game, the whole country came together to support the effort. It also brought together the diverse officers in Mandela's security team, with each respecting their colleagues' professionalism and dedication.

And when the mostly white South Africa team had an upset win over the favoured New Zealand team, the nation came together to celebrate, and the spirit of one united country was powerful. It's a day that South Africa will not forget for a long,

long time. Mandela held firm in his belief that the Springboks could achieve the unthinkable, and he made absolutely sure every single player shared his belief.

The Springboks did it once again in 2019, fighting their way through to the finals facing the team from England that had just delivered a shocking upset to the famed All-Blacks from New Zealand. The wind was at the back of the English team, but they were about to go toe-to-toe with a team from South Africa led by their captain, Siya Kolisi. His was a story of enduring a life of poverty, losing his mother at the age of 15 and overcoming many challenges to secure the prestigious role as captain of the Springboks. His story had inspired the nation, and his teammates rallied around his selfless, humble approach to leadership. He was fiercely committed to the game, to his teammates and his mission to prove that with commitment, determination and hard work, anyone can make their dreams come true. And he did just that on a balmy autumn afternoon in Japan, leading the South Africans to a convincing win over the team from England. In the process, Kolisi became the first-ever black captain of a rugby team to win the World Cup. He fought hard, overcame challenges and led his team to victory, and he left no doubt.

Now, back to your own journey. You've started to create a conversation with your audience. By sharing your vision, you've reaffirmed it in your own heart and mind. And, as you continue to share your version of the future, it's also important to beware of the Chinese Whispers trap. Most of us fall into it at some point or the other. The message we share on stage can sometimes be interpreted and shared in a very different way off stage. Lack of clarity and misunderstanding of the message can sabotage your vision.

And that brings me back to the importance of consistency. Leaders need to remain laser sharp and focused when expressing the vision and to protect the message at all costs, and not to deviate. The words you choose to express yourself may differ, along with the environment, but the message must be the same. Protect the core at all times. The message should not be diluted nor distorted as it passes from ear to ear.

Recently, I had dinner with a CEO of a large multinational company who shared a real example of how the message can get distorted as it changes hands. The statement at his leadership team meeting was, "We will focus on delivery, great service, honouring our passion for continuous improvement while sustaining profitability and growth …" but by the time it reached the water cooler his message somehow became, "We will focus on delivering profit."

He was caught by surprise at a companywide town hall shortly after the leadership team had met offsite when someone asked, "Why are we shifting toward a priority solely focused on profit?" His message had been altered to the point where it was unrecognizable. He then spent considerable time and effort rolling back the misinterpretation and setting the record straight. And this slowed down the momentum of the organization to move toward the original vision as the CEO had expressed to his leaders. It's therefore vital to protect the message and deliver it in a way that is consistent in its passion to excite.

We also know that as the demographics change, the message needs to change too. Not in the content, but in the how of the delivery. Millennials and the Gen Z workforce have grown up in a world of connectivity. They also live in a universe where they communicate through 'bits and bytes.'

Some say the young 'Z's have a short attention span. I am not sure if that's true, but I can certainly tell you this. The senior leaders I have worked with – myself included – all have increasingly short attention spans. This is not surprising at all, considering the sheer volume of information we deal with every day. We simply cannot afford the time to spend on every single issue that comes our way. We need to be quick in our decision-making, especially the reflexive types of decisions based on a few key facts.

And so, if you think about building excitement, particularly among the younger team members, you need to communicate in a way that resonates with them. Ultimately, these two generations are attracted to purpose and cause, and they are the ones who will carry your vision forward and ensure it's sustainable. The message should be sharp and relevant and be presented in their language. The younger generations tend to be ambitious. They ask questions like, "How can I make an impact?" "How can I be a part of the greater purpose?" "How can I change the world?" These questions are very important to them. As leaders, we need to provide the answers to their questions before they're asked.

The same rule holds true for those team members in the middle or nearing the end of their careers. Understanding what motivates them and how they communicate is a crucial trigger to ensuring your vision is digested and ignites a sense of excitement and belief, which then leads to action.

Impactful leaders know that excitement is not built through buckets of information or multiple PowerPoint slides. It's more like an IV drip, a consistent message, presented with a regular cadence, feeding small chunks of communication that can be easily digested. This is where most leaders could do with some help and coaching.

TIPS: EXCITE TO IGNITE THE FLAME

Use the power of language.

Abraham Lincoln is commonly referred to as the 'poet president.' His Gettysburg Address, one of the most powerful and stirring speeches, was just 272 words long. Its ending, "*and that government of the people, by the people, for the people, shall not perish from the earth*"[14] remains the most inspiring clarion call for democracy. He inspired an entire nation to action, and he did it in about ten sentences.

Emphasize the words that matter.

Be careful to avoid being **too bold**. We've all been subjected to emails or internal newsletters that are filled with bold fonts and capital letters to emphasize what the writer sees as the most important points of the message. This can have the opposite effect, as most people tune out when the message is too loud.

Be authentic, optimistic, with conviction and inspire the team to believe. Talk about a power-packed example of how to express!

Take advantage of the brief window.

The average adult has an attention span of 10–12 minutes. This is the window where you have the full attention of your audience – grab it fast. It's the magical moment when you have the potential to inspire to action. Miss the chance and you've lost them. As JFK's speechwriter[15] so beautifully coined the requirements of a good speech, "clarity, brevity, levity and charity!"

Leave the audience looking for more.

As every experienced public speaker or stand-up comedian knows well, always leave them wanting more. Address the most important points but leave room for questions like, "What's next?" or better yet, "When can we start?" There is an old joke that the large majority of people clap for a presentation because it's over. You want them to clap because they are looking for more.

Dave McKay had an interesting challenge when he took over as president and CEO of the Royal Bank of Canada (RBC) in 2014. Having led this Toronto-based financial services giant with great success in their personal and commercial banking division, McKay's credentials were impeccable.

McKay's challenge came from a different direction, though. His iconic predecessors had successfully navigated RBC to the leading position in the industry. And, as often happens, holding the pole position led to a culture of entitlement and complacency. How could he introduce a sense of hunger and excitement to an organization that was content in their success? How could he energize them through a new vision of agile innovation? Dave McKay knew that satisfaction with the status quo would

EXCITEMENT COMES FROM THE OPPORTUNITY TO BE PART OF SOMETHING SPECIAL.

EXCEPTIONAL LEADERS BRING *SOMETHING SPECIAL.*

prove to be the biggest threat to the future of RBC. His words summed up the brutal facts: "I want RBC to matter – to our clients, to our people and in our communities – both here in Canada and around the world, wherever we do business."[16]

'Collective ambition.' This was McKay's mantra in achieving his vision. He placed organizational purpose at the heart of RBC's business model. He powerfully articulated the 'why' of RBC's existence, starting with the creation of the 'RBC Collective Ambition Champions Group.' He talked about leadership as a collective accountability. He assembled a group of diverse leaders that became his sounding board, the early advocates and influencers. His 'Vision and Values Jam' session had more than 20,000 people from 22 countries to share collective excitement through more than 17,000 threads of communication flow. The evangelists emerged as a result and spread his message.

In a short period of time under McKay's leadership, RBC found its new mojo "to be among the world's most trusted and successful financial institutions." And 80,000 employees across the world had a renewed energy and excitement, which gave RBC a new thrust forward.

Confronting brutal facts with transparency along with the team is a great way to ensure that people start thinking about the challenge as their problem, and one that requires a collective effort to resolve and rise above. It's up to the leader to stand in front of the mirror, gather the team around and look at the problem together. The humility and the sense of the *leader as human* that this action demands is extremely powerful.

One of the traps we can fall into as leaders is to look at the excitement piece of leadership as largely transactional, a series of boxes that need to be ticked. For example:

- We have created the compelling vision according to the E5 template – this box is ticked.
- We've come up with an omnichannel strategy as recommended by my marketing function, including blogs, vlogs, town halls, one-on-ones, great conversations – this box is ticked.
- We are adhering to set schedules, and we are delivering the message to our people as per the plan – another box ticked.

Unfortunately, that's not the formula for impactful leadership, let alone inspirational leadership. To take it to the next level, aspirational leadership is all about delivering the essence and the passion of the vision with maximum impact to encourage the team to reach higher.

Something that has fascinated me for some time is the ability of outstanding leaders to shift seamlessly between inspirational and aspirational leadership. Inspirational leaders get people excited, and they can do so with just about any topic. Aspirational leaders, on the other hand, provoke people to dream, to raise the bar, to be better. This isn't about choosing one over the other; it's about merging one into another at different points in exciting your people. Both have different drivers, for sure, but they have the potential to create huge excitement.

In the context of the E5, we have seen that a clear vision of what you stand for and where you are going is vital to success. Through active listening, showing genuine interest and inclusiveness, you connect with your people on another level. Now, can you add a dash of the aspirational element? Like getting them to *want* to be better than yesterday, to aspire to be the best? Or to be known for the highest standards of excellence that others will follow?

In order for each of the five Es to be successful, the leader has to put his heart and soul – in fact, I would say, heart, soul, mind and muscle – into it. All three should come together, and this has to be refined continuously. Bringing together the inspirational and aspirational aspects allows not just you as the leader to do so, but emboldens and empowers your people to do so too.

The more you are in front of your team, the more time you spend with them, in groups or one-to-one, you start to see reactions. Add the reach of social media, where responses and reactions come in so quickly, and it's as close to a live pulse check as you'll get.

It's also very important to think of the **express** phase as something to trigger the sense of excitement that then leads to action. And this will happen only if you establish a deep connect with your people first. So how does the leader build that strong connection with the team? It starts with being authentic in your message. As we saw earlier, nobody gets emotional about jargon. Don't be wordy, get to the point and make your message relevant to the audience. Be a storyteller and make your story personal. When you do so, you will find your team leaning in, becoming attracted to the message. And in time, they will want to be part of it.

Another helpful way to ensure that you're connecting effectively is to simply ask your team how they're doing, a sort of calibration. For example, whenever I finish delivering my two-year vision presentation to my teams, I ask this question: "Okay, let's push pause now. You've heard a lot from me today. Tell me, what sticks out in your mind. What touches you? What will you take home with you today from this presentation?"

It's very insightful to hear the answers to these questions. I find that certain phrases I used and certain slides which I presented were more impactful than others. Not all aspects of my message went quite how I intended – nor were they received quite the way I had intended. The live feedback from the floor then becomes a valuable opportunity to refocus and calibrate, just in time to tweak the message for the next presentation.

Excite is really the turning point in the journey of the E5. This is the make-or-break point. Each of the Es has a clear and direct impact on bringing the vision to life. But if a leader cannot excite and inspire the team to action, the vision simply becomes a daydream.

Let's take a look at what happens once the team is excited about the vision and ready to step up to move the wheel.

GOLDEN NUGGETS
EXCITE

Excite is the first big moment of truth on the path to game-changing leadership.

The key objective of excite is to inspire people to take action.

Seize the moment. Paint a compelling picture of the future, talk about the greater purpose and the impact.

Connect with the audience early. Use their language.

Address the question, "What's in it for me?"

Help your team feel they are part of something special and that *they are special.*

Measure the excitement level by simply asking the team. Ask: "What excites you about the vision?"

CHAPTER 6

ENABLE

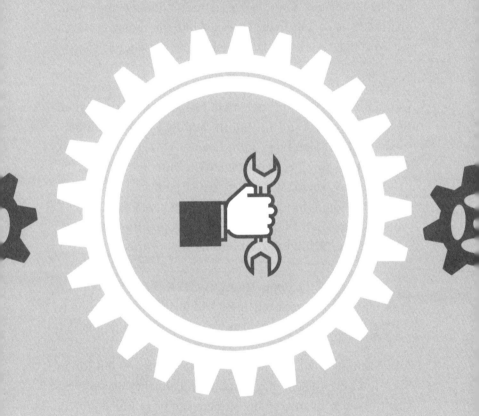

This is what transforms an idea and vision
into a movement with followership.

I t was 9 February 1964, 8pm in New York City.

For music lovers, this date and time marked a truly historical event. It was the night The Beatles made their US TV debut on *The Ed Sullivan Show*. Watched by 70 million people, with nearly 60% of all TVs in the US tuned into this moment, it set a record at that time as the largest television audience in history.

Here were four young men, on the verge of a level of fame that would prove to be unprecedented. Just months earlier, when they were living hand-to-mouth, huddled into a cramped, trashy hotel in Hamburg, John Lennon would run the boys through their routine. According to the other members of the band, Lennon would say: "'Where are we goin', fellas?' And we'd go, 'To the top, Johnny!' And he'd say, 'Where's that, fellas?!' And we'd say, 'To the toppermost of the poppermost, Johnny!' And he'd say, 'Riiiiight!' And we'd all sort of cheer up."[17]

"Toppermost of the poppermost" – this was their vision and their mantra to infuse excitement and inspiration – especially during their early days of struggle, rejection and doubt.

John Lennon, Paul McCartney, George Harrison and Ringo Starr not only created magic in their music, they also proved that the whole of an accomplishment can be so much greater than the sum of its parts. Each of them was good enough to outshine the other. Yet, instead of letting it become a polarizing factor, they embraced their individual brilliance as an 'enabling' force to create magic concert after concert, album after album.

In their very first appearance on *The Ed Sullivan Show*, they sent a clear message to the world. Breaking from the usual stage arrangement, Ringo's drum kit was raised above the stage, making him an equal centre of attention on par with the other members of the band. And, in the process, the clear line of sight helped catapult a virtually unknown drum kit brand, Ludwig, into a global leader in the industry for decades to follow. Talk about low-cost, high-impact product placement!

This was an ensemble of leaders, each in their own right, as part of a greater purpose. They shared their energy and their dream through their music, in the way they behaved both on and off the stage. Their energy was infectious and the followership that they generated was astounding. Each member had his own natural brilliance. Four individual talents, and some quirky and complementary characters, coming together, aligned toward a common goal. And having fun along the way. It's no wonder, then, that their execution was nearly perfect.

Enable. This is the critical E, the turning point where the wheels really start to move. Your compelling vision has been expressed and it has touched the hearts and minds of your team. And now there is excitement, and a sense of optimism and belief is being born. Your team is standing up, and some members are even saying, "Let's do this!" as they reach for the tools.

This is where the leader as enabler steps up. In order to harness and ignite this energy that you've worked so hard to create up until this point, it's crucial to ensure the team has the necessary tools required to bring the vision to life. But you need to move

THE GAME-CHANGING LEADER IS AN ENABLER.

MAKE SURE YOUR TEAM HAS THE RIGHT TOOLS TO ACHIEVE THEIR MISSION.

fast because that energy won't last long if there is no progress. Progress brings momentum, momentum brings success, and success brings energy.

Let's roll up our sleeves and look at ways to add **enable**, the fourth E, into our leadership arsenal.

One of the many valuable lessons I learned from my father was about the importance of having the right tools on hand. His workbench was fully stocked with extensive tools, socket wrenches and drill bits in every size and diameter available, drawers full of nails, screws and nuts and bolts of all shapes and sizes. And, needle-nose and wide pliers, Allen wrenches, hammers, screwdrivers, saws, hinges and assorted types of glue. After many years of trial and error, he had assembled the tools required to do just about any job around the house. My dad would wisely say, as he wanted me to try to remove a nail from a wall board, "Use the right tool, son, it will be much easier and you'll get the job done right."

This notion of the leader as an enabler is about focusing your energy less on doing and more on providing the tools for others to do. This presents a dilemma for most leaders. Because, let's face it, we all believe deep down that we can do the job better. I mean, that's why you're in the position as the leader, right? Someone saw that you had the magic sauce, the ability to get stuff done, to move the needle and to make an impact. And so you were placed in a position to lead people.

This is exactly where many high performers fail as leaders. The transition from someone who does to someone who enables others to do, is a big leap. But this is the stuff that outstanding leadership is made of. The leader as enabler is equivalent to the Jedi warrior moving to the level of Jedi master. As the wise leader Yoda said to his student, "Pass on what you have learned, Luke."

Every leader I've met can identify at least one person who has been instrumental in their growth as a leader. For some, it's their mother or father, for others it's a former boss, teacher or coach. What's the one common denominator here? These people are seen as mentors, and mentors do something very special. They guide us. The mentor helps us discover new ideas and find solutions to the tough problems we face. They provide advice when we come to a fork in the road and are not sure which way to go. They act as role models; they walk the talk. They are enablers.

So, what does leader as enabler really mean? As we learned earlier, it begins by crafting a compelling vision, a crystal-clear North Star, which is rooted in purpose. The leader sets the course and ensures that everyone is on board. As momentum builds, excitement follows. And then the reality of the enormous challenge ahead becomes increasingly clear. It's at this pivotal moment when the enabling leader plays a crucial role.

The enabler ensures that the environment is right for success by setting a positive 'can do, will do' tone in language and behaviour. The leader creates a culture of success. They ensure that the team has the necessary tools and skills to get the job done. But, more importantly, the enabling leader interacts with the team from a stance of support. Being an enabler sometimes means challenging and pushing the team harder, or getting them to slow down to speed up, or it simply may mean showing empathy when things aren't going according to plan or being the first to give a high-five when they are.

The enabling leader is fiercely committed to bringing the vision to life and will ensure that the team has the right tools to do this. Sometimes these tools are rooted in technology, but certainly not limited to the fancy stuff. Enabling the team to bring the vision to reality may be about the skills required to make it happen. The enabling leader identifies the competencies required to achieve success, and then ensures that every member of the team has those skills.

As you craft your vision, in parallel, this is the time to list the tools and skills required to bring the vision to life and action. The next step is to take an inventory of the team, their skill sets and the tools on hand. Out of this process, an enabling plan is born.

Enable is what transforms an idea and vision into a movement with followership. And the role of a leader as an enabler involves asking important questions:

- What are the barriers that are getting in the way of your team to achieve the goal? As a game-changing leader, you need to address this important question early on in the enable stage. Identify the barriers quickly and remove them.
- What are the tools and support systems that will help turbocharge your team's efforts to accomplish their mission?

In short, you need to inject the magic dust of enablement that will help your team accelerate to the next E– **execute**.

It's important to consider both the tangibles and the intangibles when you think about enabling.

It may be something as simple as development programmes for the team. Or it could be specific knowledge or a skill set that needs to be imported from outside. The nontangible aspects of enablement include how you behave as an enabling leader, your attitude toward mistakes and setbacks, and how you lead the team to bounce back. It is about the way you foster a sense of camaraderie on your team, and how you promote your people's wellbeing, putting your people first in everything you do, while staying firmly committed to the vision.

So, let's rewind for a moment on your progress. You've taken your compelling vision to the team in an omnichannel manner. The greater purpose of the vision has hit the bullseye in peoples' hearts and minds, it answers their 'why' with unerring precision. And it paints a vivid picture of what success will look like. People are excited and showing signs of being inspired to action. Some are actually getting off their seats and saying things like, "When do we start?" and "Let's do this." You can feel the signs of a movement beginning to emerge.

Now, what's the quickest way to bring this movement to a complete stop, to extinguish the aspirational fire? You guessed it. By being the leader who gets the team fired up, says 'go' and then fades away into the corner office, door closed. By not engaging with the team nor enabling them with the right tools to execute on the vision, the sense of excitement and eagerness quickly dissolves.

We'll talk more later about how to engage effectively with the team. Let's focus for now on the tools. How do you really know what the right tools are to provide for your team? This question should be addressed well before you reach the enable stage. In fact, the game-changing leader needs to start this exercise in parallel with crafting the vision. As you identify your North Star and create the compelling story around the purpose, you need to come down to the ground and think about how you'll help the team get there, and create a list of the tools that are required when you shift into the stage of leader as enabler.

And this is where the interdependence of the five Es kicks in. While I've presented the five Es in a particular order, it's also important to know that they are independent of and interdependent on each other. Which means, once you've gone through the Es one by one, there's no rigid order that you must follow in the second round.

Shouldn't there be a vision before we talk about the other Es, you may ask? The vision, the goal or the objective is indeed the starting point. It's the North Star – the basis of the entire discussion of the E5. Get the vision right, touch hearts and minds, and the rest will flow naturally.

And that is why it's important to move into the action phase only when you've gone through the E5 sequence and ticked the important boxes. Before you even step out on the floor to share the vision, you should ask yourself: "What are the tools we will need to execute on this vision?" "What are the tools that we are missing?"

Enabling also means having the right people to leverage the tools you'll provide. The tough question needs to be asked at the very beginning, as you craft your vision: "Do we have the right people for the journey ahead? Do we have the right people, with the right skills?" And then weave your way and simulate through each of the Es. Your laundry list of tools will emerge. At the **enable** stage, take an inventory of what's in your toolbox and what's not.

Leading transformation begins with assembling the right people. Unfortunately, many leaders set out on the game-changing journey with the wrong people and the wrong skill sets, ill-prepared for the challenge ahead or, even worse, people with the wrong values. It's important to address this and make the tough decisions before you reach the **enable** stage. If you don't have the necessary skills in your team, you have a choice: develop them in your current team or import the skills and knowledge from outside.

Principle #1
Don't wait for the curtain to rise on the **enable** stage to think about the tools needed. Plan for this at the **envision** stage and have them ready to go before the team is inspired to action. Provide the tools and step out of their way!

Principle #2
Make sure you have the right people to leverage these tools. The team member who is missing the necessary skills can be

a disabler. Add in someone with questionable values and you have a potent mix that will sabotage your efforts to bring your compelling vision to life. This is a moment of truth for the game-changing leader. It requires courage to make tough decisions, to confront the brutal facts, and accept that the team is missing an important skill required to achieve the vision. The enabling leader must be prepared to show courage.

Recently I had a tough conversation with a CEO who was struggling with the performance of his CFO. The company had grown quickly over the past five years, nearly tripling in revenue and scope. The CFO had joined a much smaller organization and was performing well within that scope. But the role now required a different type of leader with a wider set of skills, especially a higher level of strategic thinking. The CFO was a loyal soldier, someone who followed the processes as laid out by the leader. As we talked about the CEO's vision, we did a deep dive into the skills required by the members of the senior leadership team in order to lead the respective teams toward bringing the vision to reality. We did an inventory, listing up the three or four most crucial skills required from each leader.

The conclusion was clear: the CFO had fulfilled his purpose and performed his duties to the best of his abilities ... but the organization had evolved and grown faster than the CFO. It was time for him to graduate, to move on, allowing the CEO to bring in someone better prepared to take the organization into the future.

It's important to take regular stock of the overall capabilities of your team and ask the tough questions. Do they have what it takes to lead the team or make an impact into the day after tomorrow? Too many leaders hire for today, based on a burning platform, a hole to fill. Transformational leaders peek around the corner and identify the qualities required to bring the organization into the future, and to the front of the pack. And like any winning sports coach knows well, the skills required to get there are diverse. But perhaps just as important as the skills the team possesses is the character mix of the team, from conservative to bold, from cautious to aggressive, with a maverick or two added to the mix to keep things exciting.

In order to ignite the potential of the maverick, it's important to understand that their intense passion to make an impact is partly rooted in their innate desire to pursue goals that they set for themselves. They don't see themselves as breaking rules, but instead as charting a creative path to deliver success. They have an amazing ability to bounce back from failure, and they do it with resilience and conviction. Mavericks don't necessarily rebel against the company or their managers. What they do is fight anything that gets in the way of achieving their goals.

Leading the maverick requires four key strategies:
1. Ensure that the vision is crystal clear with a heavy focus on the 'why.'
2. Give them space to exercise independent and innovative thinking under the premise that no idea is a bad idea.
3. Create a safe zone for healthy disagreements. Protect and encourage them, remove misconceptions of right and wrong, and of winners and losers.

4. Allow them to fail fast and move on. The maverick's biggest strength is their resilience, and the appetite to take risks amid volatility and uncertainty – the prospect of possible failures does not faze them.

Research, combined with my own first-hand experience, has taught me that diverse teams are stronger teams. We need hunters and farmers, those who think and those who jump, with a few mavericks in the mix to keep things exciting. We need the aggressive types, just as we need the reflective thinkers, the protectors. When the leader shifts into the enabling mode, a key objective is to ensure that the team has the right mix of personalities, skills, knowledge and tools required to execute on the vision. Once the right people with the right tools are assembled, you're ready for action. But to ensure that the action leads to strong execution, it's crucial to come up with a mechanism to ensure the team is indeed moving in the direction of your North Star.

There are two very effective tools that I've used in my own organizations over the years. The first is what I call the pulse check. The **pulse check** is really about getting your finger on the pulse of your people. As a leader, you need to have a clear sense of the heartbeat of your team. Are they heading in the right direction? Are they motivated? Are they confident? Is there growing momentum or dissent? And you need to know this early on so you can either add fuel to the fire or intervene to ensure the team gets back on track. In the early stages of a new initiative or project, I hold these pulse checks with the key leaders of the teams once a week. It's a brief meeting,

normally 15–20 mins maximum held on Mondays, where
important, open-ended questions are asked:

- How was the past week?
- What prevented you from moving forward last week?
  (if applicable)
- What's your objective this week?
- What support do you need to make it happen?
- How is the team doing?

Often, it's the last question that's the most revealing, and
depending on your preference, this question can be asked right
up front. Over a few weeks of holding the pulse check, you'll start
to see a pattern emerge. Of course, any leader will have good
and bad weeks, but what you're really looking for is whether
the team is moving the wheels in the right direction, and if the
leader is consistent in their effort to enable the team. The pulse
checks also help create a strong sense of followership when the
leader speaks to fellow leaders as a peer. In the process, you'll
start to see evangelists emerge, the leaders who are passionate
and committed to bringing the vision to life. The evangelist will
become an important part of your efforts to enable the team.

The second tool that is effective in keeping teams on track
is the **compass meeting**. We discussed the compass offsite
earlier, and this is the follow-up cadence. The compass meeting
is made up of leaders and their direct reports, and the key
enabling business partners for the team (HR, finance, IT, etc.).
Some would call it a business review, but there is a difference. The compass meeting begins with revisiting the North
Star and the pillars, which guide the team toward the goal.

The discussion begins with reaffirming the direction, and then shifts into progress since the last meeting, and then to people. The compass meeting should not begin with numbers or metrics. The objective of this meeting is to ensure that the team is not only heading in the right direction, but also at the right pace. And to identify any potential red flags around barriers to accelerate, both internal and external. Depending on the team and the situation, compass meetings may be held weekly or monthly. For the teams that are just starting out on the journey or those that are lacking direction or showing weak traction, the compass meeting is held once a week.

You can create your own version of the pulse check and the compass meeting aligned to your vision and driven by your mission to enable. One piece of advice: if you truly aspire to be a game-changing leader, you need to be present at these meetings, at least in the early stages. Engaged leaders make it their priority to be in the game.

It sounds simple, but it's so crucial. You cannot be at 30,000 feet to be in the game. As a leader, I would recommend you attend the touchpoint meetings you set up with your teams to enable them. Over time, your team will start to show momentum, progress and results in moving toward the vision. At this point, you may loosen the grip a little and let them have the freedom to move. Some may view this as micromanagement. Far from it. In fact, it's about giving what we saw earlier in the book, something that Dan Cable calls "freedom in the frame."

We know that it's crucial for the leader to be engaged and in touch with the team. This means being present with your people: to observe, to prompt, and to provoke them to activate their 'seeking system' (as Dan Cable terms it in his book, *Alive at Work*) and to encourage them to move with freedom. In the process, you'll ignite their problem-solving skills. This frame gets bigger as they earn your trust through momentum and the performance that it generates. And then the virtuous cycle begins. You further enable them by allowing them to grow as they experiment within the bigger frame. It's an extremely effective and enabling technique, and it's made possible because you're present.

Being present means you're *all in*. To borrow a term that is commonly used, being *all in* means the need to be *mindful*. The enabling leader is fully engaged in the moment, not preoccupied with other thoughts. Your inner conversations on issues unrelated to the team in front of you are briefly switched off. You're in the moment and the team has 100% of your attention. A difficult task, considering the challenges of constant disruption, which we talked about earlier. It's tough to be mindful when our minds are so full.

Thanks to text messages, social media and email, our 'to-do list' seems to grow out of control from the moment we wake up each day. Being in the moment then, takes real effort, but it's well worth it. The more your thoughts and actions are centred around your people, the more they will be engaged. And, ultimately, engaged teams move the needle.

High-performing teams are self-motivated and self-regulating. They don't require the leader to guide them each step of the way.

The leader as the all-knowing, almighty power, the one with all the answers, is gone. With an immense amount of information on just about any topic easily accessible via a quick search on the internet, the era of the leader as the sage, the one who possesses the knowledge, has ended. What people are looking for today is a leader who will set a clear direction and get them excited about it, while enabling them to score goals along the way.

Your team is ready to roll up their sleeves, get their hands dirty and to do the hard work. They look to you as their leader who can help identify and remove the bottlenecks that are slowing them down. They see you as the 'turbocharger leader' who will inject, from time to time, that vital fuel required to accelerate their momentum. Some call this 'servant leadership,' but I'm not a big fan of the term. The leader is not simply there to serve the team. Instead they are fully present, working with the team shoulder to shoulder and engaged on a mission to enable. Because, when all is said and done, the leader won't lead the execution, the team will.

When it comes to choosing enablers for our teams, leaders are easily mesmerized by technology. We can easily fall into the trap of assuming that the latest technology is the enabler. Be careful – technology can be as much an enabler as it can be a disabler.

We've all been there. How about the time when you looked at a certain technology (say, a CRM system), believing it would revolutionize your business? Help you communicate better with your customers? Or make your team more streamlined in the way they approach the market and execute on your account planning? But in the end, the tool either proved to be a distraction or was simply ineffective. Tools are only as good as the user. This is because implementing a new tool also involves a change in behaviour that drives the new tool. The same behaviour with a new tool gives the same, or even worse, results.

Game-changing leadership starts with behaviour. Technology is just one of the many effective tools in the armoury. But technology is driven by people. So, make sure you have the right people. Game-changing leaders anticipate change. They gather facts and opinions and observe trends. They come up with a hypothesis based on a combination of these facts and opinions, and then make a decision.

For instance, we have launched the 'Day After Tomorrow' strategy for our leadership team. Like any industry, the HR services and staffing industry is highly competitive and changing fast. On many levels, the world is becoming increasingly commoditized and the competitive landscape is constantly taking new shapes with disruptors entering the space almost daily. With this unprecedented speed of change (especially in an environment like India, which is literally under construction!), it became clear to me that we needed to stop talking about today, or even tomorrow for that matter.

Rik Vera, a well-known futurist and author of *Managers The Day After Tomorrow*,[18] tells the story of companies, and entire industries, which fell behind because they were too focused on the moment. They had the right tools for today, but those tools would soon become obsolete. Others were already using the tools designed for the future, and these organizations had put in place a future-focused strategy that leveraged those tools for acceleration. The winning organizations were preparing for the day after tomorrow.

We took this notion to our leaders under the theme of DAT (Day After Tomorrow). Leaders across all business and support functions were brought together for the annual strategic offsite. Typically, the flow is predictable: opening context is set by the CEO, financial report from the CFO, presentations from HR, marketing and IT, with breakout sessions scattered in between. Not this time. We mixed it up; we started the day with logos of companies that missed the bus, starting with Kodak. And then on one slide, a compelling question in big bold letters:

WHAT ARE YOU DOING NOW TO PREPARE YOUR TEAM FOR THE DAY AFTER TOMORROW?

The silence that followed was the harsh answer. Our leaders viewed tomorrow as next month, next quarter, the rest of the financial year. They weren't climbing up the tree to look at the landscape, nor were they preparing their teams to be ahead of the curve. By the time we wrapped up the two-day session, every leader in the room had crafted a DAT plan, with the follow-up commitment to gather their teams to dissect and digest it, and to come up with an action plan to bring it to life. The E5 was activated.

Fast forward 12 months … new milestones and best-ever milestones have been achieved across the four corners of the organization, and DAT has become part of our daily vocabulary in leadership team meetings and even at the water cooler. Just imagine the potential of an organization made up of leaders who are fully in the game today, with a crystal-clear plan to lead their teams into the day after tomorrow. In a way, by introducing the concept of DAT planning, we further enabled the teams to bring our vision to life.

Here's an analogy: look at your team as sticks of dynamite. As the game-changing leader it's your job to place the dynamite in all the right spots around your organization. Then, it's up to you as the leader to bring fire to the party and ignite the dynamite. This fire comes in many shapes and forms. Sometimes it's a match, and other times it's a blowtorch. These are your enablers. Once you've placed the dynamite in the right spots, light the fire together with your evangelists, the most committed and passionate members of the team, and then watch out! The multiplier effect kicks in and … boom! The enablers that you carefully choose and place ignite explosions which help to sustain momentum. And these lead to the ultimate moment of truth – **execution**.

Earlier in the chapter on **enable**, we talked about the vital need for the leader to be in touch, to have a 'mindful presence.' Repeating the message, there's really no substitute for face time with your team and coming to understand their barriers.

Once we identify what they are, we can start the process of removing those barriers and truly enable our teams.

Crafting a strong vision, sharing it and getting people excited about it are key steps leading toward effective execution. But the moment of truth comes when the leader digs in, walks the talk, removes barriers and goes to any length to ensure that the team delivers beyond expectations. Ensuring that they have everything they need to achieve the task raises the leader's stature and credibility. They become powerful magnets of followership.

When I turn the E5 model on myself and look in the mirror, one thing is clear: of all the five Es, **enable** is my weakness. I have a hard time identifying how I can best enable the team to move forward. And so, it's the E that I work on the most. In fact, this realization led me to create the pulse check and compass meeting approach.

But nobody is a master of all of the five Es. Just as our teams are made up of diverse people with different skills and personalities, each of us as leaders are unique animals. We need to look in the mirror and be honest with ourselves, identify our strengths and weaknesses when it comes to each of the five Es and seek out support where needed. Of course, we naturally gravitate to the Es that we enjoy, the ones we are good at. In turn, we tend to avoid or perhaps even ignore the Es that make us feel awkward or fit outside our comfort zone. This tendency to avoid uncomfortable topics or situations is something that game-changing leaders are acutely aware of, and make a strong effort to do the opposite and instead to address the elephant in the room. And leaders should surround themselves with their own enablers.

IT'S AT THE *ENABLE* STAGE THAT THE LEADER'S RESILIENCE IS PUT TO THE TEST.

THIS IS THE TIME FOR TOUGH DECISIONS.

KNOW **YOURSELF**

I need help with **enable**, so I ask for it. Leaders should surround themselves with their own enablers. Typically, in an organization, it can be the CFO, head of IT or the head of HR. So, I'm close to all my functional leaders who have the expertise. I get their advice and their support to enable the team to deliver on the vision that we jointly crafted. It's been a very useful approach and, frankly, humbling as well. It has also helped to create a stronger sense of followership in the team as they observe their leader as human.

Let's assume you've succeeded in exciting your team through your expression of a compelling vision. You've done an inventory of the enablers required, the potential disablers and the triggers to accelerate momentum toward achieving the vision.

And then, you discover that while some team members are moving forward at a good pace and have leverage the enablers provided, others are not. What should you do when someone understands the vision, is excited about it, has the required tools to achieve its execution but is still not making progress? Or, in the worst case, the team member is not solidly on board and has made little, if any, progress. In both cases, the game-changing leader steps up.

First, it's important for the team to not only know where they're going but also to understand how progress will be measured. The evidence of progress must be measurable, capable of being validated and incremental. The leader should expect progress, with clear and identifiable steps forward toward bringing the vision to life.

When progress is lacking, it's time to dig deeper, starting with behaviours among the team members who are lagging. Here is a checklist of items to look for:

- Do they have a clear understanding of the vision, the greater purpose and the North Star?
- Do they have the tools and know how to use them?
- Do they have full support from colleagues and managers?
- Do they appear to be committed to bring the vision to life?

If you answer 'yes' to all of the above, it may simply be a competency issue. In which case you'll need to consider moving this person to another role. On the other hand, you may see evidence of 'blame' behaviours. For example, you hear words like, "It's the market" or "It's the IT team's fault" or "HR is not getting people fast enough."

The conclusion here is simple. This person is not excited and certainly is not committed to doing what it takes to bring your vision to reality. In the process, the person could threaten to slow down the momentum you've worked so hard to create. One of the key responsibilities of the leader is to be aware when someone becomes a disabler, and the leader should be ready to take the courageous step of removing them. Here is where the pulse check comes in handy. It helps to understand who is consistent and who is not, as well as who is moving forward and who remains in the same place. When you remove the disabler from the team, you're sending out a clear message and drawing a line in the sand that opting out is simply not an option.

Strong leadership requires the ability to build followership. Traditionally, when we talk about leadership, we refer to the leader at the front. The followers, on the other hand, are assumed to be the people standing beside or behind the leader. However, as leaders, we come to realize that we need to be capable of taking different positions in the teams we lead.

The enabling leader sometimes needs to be a leader positioned at the front, as the pace setter. At times, they need to be at the side, as the adviser and cheerleader. At other times, they need to be positioned behind the group, as an enabler. The leader must also, on occasions, be in the middle as a player. As a leader from above, it's about being strategic. From below, the leader plays the role of supporter. Being able to and knowing when to play each role is one clear difference between a competent manager and an exceptional leader.

Enabling is a 4D phenomenon. Knowing when to be at the front or at the side, and when to move to the middle and back – this is crucial. And it's not just about positioning. *Being there* is simply not enough to move the needle. The impactful leader knows when to push and when to pull. Another way to put it – these leaders know when to shift from being the pace setter at the front, to being the enabler by the side, and the supporter at the back. They move from role to role seamlessly. This is really the craft, the blend of art and science that merge to form the core of great leadership.

We all have good days and bad days; it's the nature of being human. As an enabling leader, it's important not to make rash decisions about people. However, when someone is giving support and coaching but continues to show inconsistency in performance and commitment, a tough decision has to be made.

The tough questions need to be asked: "Does this person have the right values for our organization?" Assuming the answer is 'yes,' the next question is this: "Can the team member be redeployed to another role where they can shine?" If the answer is 'no' to either or both the questions, the person needs to leave the organization.

In my experience, the best leaders are the ones who inspire their employees and enable them. Ultimately, the best leaders are mentors who inspire us to emulate them as leaders, even when they have to make difficult decisions. Earlier we talked about how enabling wasn't my natural strength. However, over the years, I have actively accepted help. Of course, experience has taught me valuable lessons on the leadership activities that are so important at the enable stage. And when I think about the leaders who inspired me, those who made a significant impact on me and my journey as a leader, they were the enablers. They were the leaders who helped me move forward, who supported me through good times and bad, and ensured that I had what I needed to be successful. These are the leaders who I aim to emulate so it's a bit ironic that my biggest weakness as a leader is the thing I admire most about my mentors!

TIPS: ENABLE TO BECOME A TOOL MASTER

Fill the toolbox.
If you want to get the job done right, you need to ensure your team has the right tools. Not sure what they need? Ask them.

Identify the barriers and remove them.
Being in the game means rolling up your sleeves and enabling the team. Knock down the walls that are preventing the team from accelerating.

Clarify the roles.
All high-performing teams are made of individuals with different personalities, skill sets and natural talents. Put the right people on the right task and make it crystal clear.

Celebrate milestones as the team moves forward.
It's a marathon, not a sprint. Identify milestones and celebrate them with the team. Feel pride in achieving milestones.

Open up the mic.
Encourage a culture of vigorous and healthy debate. What you don't want is a team of people with heads on hinges reluctantly working on your vision just because the boss has said so. Create opportunities for your team to push pause. Encourage them to question and debate the 'what' and the 'how.'

All for one, one for all.
Spend time with the team but be sure to spend time with each

individual who makes up the team. Put your priority on one-on-one informal chats and have some great conversations. Let them know you have their back.

Clash to collaborate.
Encourage healthy conflict, play devil's advocate, question the team with 'why?' and allow others to do the same.

Take everything seriously, take nothing personally.
Accept this fact – there will be roadblocks along the way. And it's easy to fall into the trap of taking the lack of progress as defiance by the team or as a direct reflection of your effectiveness as a leader. Don't take it personally, instead focus your energy on the mission at hand.

Coach, don't tell.
Use the skills of questioning, probing, listening and triggering 'aha' moments to make them step on the accelerator to reach the goal. Avoid yes or no questions. Prompt the team to ask each other: "What if …" "Why … ?" and "How about …?"

Back away.
The best way to suck the energy out of an eager team is to micromanage every step. Once there is clear momentum, move from being a leader at the front to leader as a guide from the side.

Be available.
As you back away, make sure you're always available and ready to support.

GOLDEN NUGGETS
ENABLE

Move from visionary and evangelist to enabler.

The wheels really gain momentum when you enable
the team with the right tools.

Go back to the envision stage, recall the tools you listed
in order to bring the vision to reality. Get those tools.

Do regular pulse checks on commitment levels.

Guide from the side – be the student.

Be present. Be in the game.

Give the team 'freedom in the frame,'
room to move and to experiment.

Be prepared to make tough decisions.

CHAPTER 7

EXECUTE

Execution is when it all comes together.
It's the moment of truth.

The recent attempt by the Indian space agency to land on the moon is a great lesson in the E5 at work.

Chandrayaan-2, as the mission was named, was an audacious vision that excited and inspired the nation of India. In an unprecedented moment, the entire country was glued to their TVs, staying awake to root for their country's achievements in science and technology, even if it didn't impact their everyday lives. The project planning and management was impeccable with the right scientists and programme managers deployed, the right tools and technologies made available for its execution.

The execution was perfect and precise as the mission moved on track until the last few minutes before the landing. Within just meters of the moon, the control station in Bangalore suddenly and inexplicably lost contact with the Vikram lander. A stunned nation watched the jam-packed control centre, filled with engineers and scientists, go from a mood of jubilation and celebration to a deafening silence, suspense and utter fear at what might come next.

True, the lander failed to achieve its mission. But there is much more to this story from a leadership perspective. The display of genuine empathy by the Indian Prime Minister Modi as he consoled and hugged a weeping Sivan, Chairman of the India Space Research Organization, was a lesson in what enabling leadership means.

It was a powerful demonstration of how a leader as an enabler can impact success. If we measure success only by the final outcome, then perhaps this mission did not qualify. On the other hand, there were several milestone successes achieved along the way in this mission. Some were 'first evers,' and some others 'best evers.' And although the objective was not fully achieved, there was more than partial success. In fact, it was declared a 98% success. These milestones are important steps forward toward achieving the bold vision. In that sense, they qualify as successes in execution. The role of the leader, in such instances, is to help the team gain perspective and revisit the vision.

Leading teams to achieve greatness is a process. Rarely does a leader create a compelling vision, express it in a way that builds excitement, enables the team with the necessary tools and then magically executes. Execution is a trial-and-error process. We try, fall, get back up, keep moving forward, learn from the bumps in the road, rally together, get stronger and smarter … and move forward. This creates a virtuous loop that will ultimately lead to success and execution of the vision.

Kaizen Meets Jugaad

In the 1990s, the Japanese word *kaizen* started to enter into the vocabulary of engineers and project managers in the manufacturing world. *Kaizen* is a concept that lies deep in the souls of the Japanese. It's about meticulous analysis of the process, breaking down the steps involved in achieving an outcome and then finding a way to improve each and every step. It begins by looking for the root cause of a problem and then asking 'why' five times. Typically, the process, like many things in Japan, is carried out by teams that identify the bottleneck, discuss and debate the 'how' to improve, and once consensus is achieved, a plan of action is created. At its core, *kaizen* is about a relentless quest to be better than yesterday, rooted in the belief that we can always be better.

On the other hand, there is a phenomenon born in India that has just recently starting to enter into the vocabulary of global leaders called *jugaad*. *Jugaad* is at the core of the spirit of Indians, a difficult word to define. It's really about ingenuity and creativity and finding a way to get things done with limited resources. Sort of like opening the fridge and deciding to make an elaborate feast without a recipe, utilizing all of the ingredients on hand. The spirit of *jugaad* is evident on every street corner in the country, with incredibly creative makeshift contraptions handcrafted to get a task done. I've witnessed first-hand as a group of Indian friends gathered around to find a way to boil water after we ran out of propane for the stove. They took an iron, put it on full heat, turned the iron upside down, carefully balanced it between two sneakers, then filled up the steel kettle and placed it on top of the hot iron. Three minutes later, a few high-5's as we were having a hot cup of chai and admiring the living proof of *jugaad* in front of us!

The execution phase requires a mix of *kaizen* and *jugaad*. That is, it's important to identify the process and milestones on the path toward bringing the vision to life. At the same time, execution requires a creative spirit, with the guts to experiment from time to time. To leverage existing resources to achieve the mission. Marrying the relentless focus of *kaizen* with the entrepreneurial spirit of *jugaad* is a powerful combination.

Successful execution requires you to keep coming back for more. As Sir Edmund Hillary asserted after an unsuccessful bid to summit Mount Everest, "I will come again and conquer you because as a mountain you can't grow, but as a human I can." This spirit of resilience, creativity, and the sheer ability to bounce back can influence others to join you. This is the stuff that outstanding leadership is made of.

THE E5: ONE FOR ALL, ALL FOR ONE

Each element of the E5 is a trigger for game-changing leadership. The Es are interdependent, and each is a necessary piece of a bigger puzzle. Each of the Es relies on another, and the synergy they produce come together to culminate in your winning formula of **execute**. This is where the vision finally becomes reality, the true measurement of great leadership.

Execute: it's when all of the thought, analysis, planning, communication and actions start to gain momentum – and then comes the moment of truth.

In the previous chapter, we talked at length about **enable**, and why it's so crucial to gaining momentum. Passionate effort has gone into crafting a compelling vision. A lot of thought and care have been invested in communicating it as an omnichannel expression. This effort has ignited excitement, and it's becoming clear that the team is inspired. And you're fuelling it all by working hard to provide your team with the right tools and support they need to move the wheels. The E5 is a process, a journey and **execute** is one important piece of the puzzle. And the revelation is that it actually began way back in the **envision** stage.

From the very beginning, the compelling vision needs to be built for execution. As a leader, visualize it. Can the vision be developed and brought to life by igniting each of the Es? Are you confident that you can enable the team to achieve? This requires two synchronous, parallel processes.

The first is visualization. This is where the leader helps the team to imagine the vision, what it looks like, the shape. The leader takes the team on a virtual journey, rooted in asking the questions: What if … ? and When we … ? The team begins to see it take shape in their imaginary world. They can see it come to life and feel the sensation when it happens.

The second is to give cognitive clarity – to stimulate your team's seeking mind, where logic meets creativity, and where envisioning and collaboration are ignited together. Out of this comes the excitement of shooting for an ambitious goal that the team concludes is absolutely achievable. And the work begins. When the leader gets these two pillars right, they become the key triggers for execution.

In my own leadership journey, I've discovered that the real moments of truth emerge when I dream about what *could be.* Asking "*What if … ?*" has become a very important part of my language with the teams I lead. It's the little voice in my head on my long morning walks when I ponder about the future and create my BHAG. The game-changing leaders I've met and studied share one common trait. They constantly ask themselves and their teams "*Why?*" and "*What if?*" And they become excited when they think about the potential impact of their bold ambition.

The '30% Club,' started in 2010 in the UK, had an ambitious vision – to increase the proportion of women on UK boards to 30 percent. Companies needed the best and brightest minds at the boardroom table and beyond, and gender balance would lead to far better outcomes – this was the compelling vision they presented to organizations. In choosing the figure of 30 percent, the cofounders of the 30% Club considered the fact that the current numbers of women on the boards of FTSE 100 companies (Financial Times Stock Exchange) was only 12.5%. Thirty percent was an ambitious target, no doubt, but doable. And it was a figure that they got board chairmen (mostly men) to enthusiastically commit to.

How did the 30% Club align its vision to execution? First, they opted for voluntary targets to obtain buy-in. They didn't choose mandated or legislated quotas. The case for change was made through deep thought and analysis of financial and sustainability performance, and economic and social development. Ultimately, the clincher was 'impact.' The '*Why*' and the '*What if*' took a central role in their ambition.

Measurable, ambitious and achievable goals were set with a defined timetable. In addition, the 30% Club leveraged an empathetic public policy that wanted the status quo to go. They elicited influencers from all walks of life to come on board and demonstrate an openness to collaborate. In the process, they ignited the multiplier effect.

Today, 14 chapters of this club across geographies relentlessly work toward achieving their goal by 2020.[19] The right enablers – investor groups, mentors, future boards schemes, business schools and leadership courses – have been made available to organizations.

To be fair, similar initiatives have been launched in other countries. In Japan, under the theme 'Womenomics'[20] similar targets were set in 2015, but the country had been unable to execute the plan. The targets were revisited and in 2019, the Japanese government, along with a consortium of the top 100 companies in Japan, decided to join the UK initiative.

It's often said that imitation is the highest form of flattery. I would say it in a different way. If someone has achieved greatness, learn from their story, and leverage it for your own effort to bring your vision to reality. There's a Latin term first recorded in the 12th century by Bernard of Chartres, *"nanos gigantum humeris insidentes,"* which is used as a metaphor to mean, "discovering truth by building on previous discoveries." Isaac Newton, in 1675, gave us a more familiar expression:[21] *"If I have seen farther it is by standing on the shoulders of giants."*

And this is exactly what the Japanese government did. They chose to put egos aside and stand on the shoulders of giants. It was an ambitious goal, considering that the participation rate stood at 6.5% as of September 2019. As of late 2019, Japan is the 14th member of the 30% Club. Based on our E5 criteria, you can say that the vision created in 2010 in the UK has now become a movement. There is excitement, and through the power of many, the enabling movement is strong. The fifth E is happening as we speak. Member nations are working hard to execute the vision, and as the collective effort gains momentum, we can expect significant progress on this important mission. These leaders have come together to change the game, to enable women to move out of the shadows and play key leadership roles.

When we talk about execution, it's very important that plans and processes are in place. But here's a word of caution. Remember, humans drive processes. Processes don't drive humans, at least not when we talk about game-changing leadership.

When facing a complicated challenge in your organization, have you ever been referred to a standard operating procedure (SOP)? The best way to kill curiosity and the seeking mind is to refer someone to a SOP. Unfortunately, many organizations turn to standardization of processes as they scale, and gradually remove the human piece from the equation. This ultimately leads the team away from innovation and transformation. Pragmatic leaders assiduously avoid this trap. They use language such as "common sense always prevails" and "the answers are in the room." While SOPs may be necessary, especially in a large organization, they should not be the default answer to every problem. When in doubt, opt for common sense.

Technology and processes do not change the game; people do. Technology and processes are simply tools to leverage in achieving the vision. In my own teams, I have a phrase that is our guiding light, especially when we hit roadblocks on the 'how' on our journey: "When in doubt, common sense should always prevail."

But here is the contradiction. Common sense is often *uncommon*. This is where the leader needs to be consistent in thought processes and behaviours. The reflexive management we talked about earlier appears when teams begin to question the 'how.'

The DISC[22] scale, a well-known personality assessment tool, says that there are four key personality profiles. The same is true for leadership profiles.

D – Dominant
I – Inspiring
S – Supportive
C – Cautious

While we are a mix of all of these elements, the game-changing leader has a high proportion of 'D' and 'I.' Leaders who are especially high on the dominant quadrant tend to get impatient with debates and discussions on the 'how.' They will often interrupt the discussion and say something like, "Okay, we've discussed this enough ... just do it!" The leader who tends to lean toward being cautious before approving plans will say, "Let's continue to discuss this, and get more opinions." Interestingly, both profiles are effective when combined, but certainly not exclusively. The danger is that the dominant leader makes rash decisions to 'just go,' often leading to radical adjustments in the strategy and losing sight of the vision. Similarly, the cautious leader tends to fall into the trap of paralysis by analysis.

There are a multitude of psychometric tools available to gauge where you and your team members fit on the personality profile scale. The Myers-Briggs Type Indicator, Gallup's StrengthsFinder, and the often-used 360-degree feedback assessment are all effective. The important thing to remember is that regardless of where we appear on the continuum, we all view the world through a unique combination of lenses. To influence and ignite action for change, it's crucial to develop the ability to view things through others' lenses.

All leadership profiles should embrace the notion of pivoting. The act of pivoting is best explained by drawing attention to riding a wave. The surfer has to carefully and attentively sense and feel his position relative to the wave he hopes to ride. No two waves come at the surfer in the same way – it sometimes slows, and sometimes speeds. Sometimes it even changes shape. An expert surfer pivots off his back foot and realigns themselves to meet the wave. And so should we too, as leaders.

By pivot, I mean to make minor adjustments. Not to overreact or decelerate momentum with knee-jerk reactions. As a leader, having the guts to pivot means checking your ego at the door. The world is changing, which means that while the premise on which we built the original vision remains firm, the environment may have changed along the way. There are simply some things we can't control in the external environment, but we do have full control over how we respond to these changes.

The seasoned leader has been through this cycle of making adjustments and slight tweaks to the tactics. The new leader tends to be more reactive, and instead of pivoting and making small tweaks, they stop and make a drastic change in direction. The zigzag path that these leaders take causes their teams to lose confidence and trust in their leader. It can also create confusion and a sense of panic. Think back to the Japanese phrase we talked about earlier. Your people are literally 'watching your back.' They will follow you if they believe you know where you're going, when you show full conviction and strong commitment to taking the team with you.

There are some fantastic examples of companies and leaders who pivoted purposefully during the execution stage. Take YouTube, for example. While it did start out as a video streaming service, it was originally meant to be a video-based dating service. 'Tune in, hook up' was their tagline as users uploaded videos to seek matches for their ideal partner. But, as they observed the behaviour of their users, they saw a pattern emerge – and an opportunity to pivot. They leveraged their original vision for their platform and transformed themselves to become a destination for video content, creating a massive community along the way to become a dominant player on a much bigger stage. They had the guts to pivot, and it paid off handsomely when they were acquired by Google for $65 billion.

Yelp is another good example of the pivot. The company's reincarnation to become the successful third-party directory it is today arose out of a pivot. In 2004, it was started as an automated platform for direct recommendations. Despite a generous funding from a PayPal cofounder, the original idea did not take off. However, an agile pivot saw it grow into a review platform. With close to 200 million reviewers in 2019, it's still growing.

It's a very good idea to enter into the **execute** stage with clear short-term goals that lead toward bringing the vision to life. By achieving milestones and celebrating them along the way, you'll create a buzz. And momentum will follow.

This leads to another moment of truth. If you told me that getting stuff done while simultaneously exciting and enabling people to reach a big hairy audacious goal is a daunting challenge, I would agree with you 100%! So how can we, as leaders, find the sweet spot of the right balance between being great at executing on the here and now, and accelerating into the day after tomorrow?

The answer lies in just three words: **BE MORE ENGAGED.**

Through the execution process, the leader needs to be more present than ever. You set the stage for the attack. The long walks in the park, the dreaming, the crafting of the vision, the expression and excitement generated in the process – all these have now led you to the action mode. You have assembled the right people with the right tools. Now it's time to roll up your sleeves with the team to execute. This is *not* the time to back away or to loosen the grip. This is the time to dig in and push the wheel, shoulder to shoulder with your team.

Many leaders fail at the execution stage. But the game-changing leader doesn't sit by and watch and wait for the game to change. These leaders get involved. They are engaged. But beware of placing a stranglehold on the team. Give the team some 'freedom in the frame.' Allow them enough room to move, to experiment, to fail, to bounce back and try again.

Freedom in the frame is freedom to *try*. The polar opposite is to micromanage. And, as we all know from our own personal experiences, nobody likes to be micromanaged. In fact, a large percentage of people leave organizations simply because of a lack of such freedom.

When the leader is involved and engaged, they naturally provide timely and frequent feedback. Timely feedback is crucial, but the frequency needs to be balanced. These great conversations should happen from a stance of support, and from the view of the leader as an enabler. The enabling leader reaches the execution stage and asks questions like: "What is getting in the way of us achieving X?" and "What can I do to help you and the team accelerate forward?"

Let's go back to our discussion on finding the sweet spot, the balance between being shoulder to shoulder with the team on the mission, while giving them the space they need to shine. When you focus your energy on execution, it becomes not just about getting things done but, more importantly, about getting the *right things* done. To this end, the enabling leader focuses on actions that help the team activate the vision. You've clarified the role for each team member with clear definitions of success, accountability and recognition in achieving milestones. You have ensured that policies, systems and processes are aligned to expected outcomes. You monitor the metrics that signify progress. And you have agility, the readiness to pivot and re-prioritize as your team works together to move the wheels.

When the wheels of execution start to gain momentum, the game-changing leader is faced with the role of becoming an accelerator and should not be a blocker. This is a challenge. Many leaders lose sight of the rocks, and the two or three most important triggers to enable the team to turbocharge their progress. Instead, they get so caught up in the process that when things aren't moving as quickly as they want, they fall into the trap of focusing on the pebbles – the small stuff, which may help the team play the game better, but won't change the game.

Identify the rocks before you start the execution phase, and don't lose sight of these crucial actions. They say the devil is in the details. But when the wheels of change start moving, being too focused on the small stuff can put the brakes on the entire operation. At the end of the day, all of us as leaders face the challenge of prioritizing and balance. Ask yourself every single day, "Is this a rock or a pebble?" Focus on the rocks, and the pebbles will take care of themselves.

When I look at my own experience in leading business transformation in Japan, Singapore, India – and, more recently, as part of a global leadership team to ignite transformation across borders – I find the execute stage to be the most exhilarating. And sometimes the most frustrating too. Sure, there are good days, when you can see signs of progress, small steps forward, hints of momentum. But there are plenty of tough days (and weeks, even months!), when you feel like there is no progress, when the plan isn't being implemented as you had intended and the energy of the team seems to be stagnant.

These moments of frustration and doubt are important moments of truth. In the face of adversity, it's crucial that leaders remain positive and stay the course. They are also a reminder that game-changing leadership is a journey that requires relentless focus, resilience and optimism. Nobody ever got up the hill without moving onward and upward.

Over history, leaders who have walked before us have left behind bits of wisdom and reflections from their own journeys. They come in proverbs, clichés and phrases. Leaders with purpose live by their own guiding principles; they have 'mantras' handy at all times. Create your own mantras and be ready to pull them out of your pocket, especially on those challenging days when you need them most!

My dad had a few of his own, and some have become my own. One of his mantras that inspires me to this day whenever I hit tough times is this: "This too shall pass." He used to say it with a big sigh, and often reached for the coffee pot and the cookie jar as he said it. A funny thing, I do exactly the same thing. There's nothing like a good cup of coffee and a chocolate chip cookie or a biscotti to make things okay.

Having faced so many challenges in his life, these four words not only helped my dad get through the tough days, but also, unknown to him, create a powerful sense of belief in our home. My brothers and our mom repeated the same message received from my dad, and it became part of our family culture. And it's no surprise that I continue to use these words with my own family today.

Game-changing leaders are interesting animals. Regardless of role, organization scope or size, public or private sector – be it in business, politics, sports or education – these leaders share one very important common trait. They have grit. This thing, grit, has been explored extensively in recent years in leadership studies and self-help books. Angela Duckworth's TED Talk: "Grit: The Power of Passion and Perseverance,"[23] is a wonderful example of how grit has been identified as a key factor in success for the high achievers among us.

Being a game-changing leader is not dependent on having a title. Titles come with assumed authority and little else. But a title on a business card or on the office door means nothing if there is no substance behind it. Followership is built through behaviours and beliefs those behaviours generate.

Baseball fans will remember this one: the 2012 Major League baseball championship. Imagine being down 0–2 games in a best

GRIT
/grɪt/

NOUN
COURAGE AND RESOLVE; STRENGTH OF CHARACTER.

"I'VE KNOWN FEW PEOPLE WHO COULD MATCH GRETA'S GRIT."

of five-series championship. Imagine staring at sudden-death elimination in Game 3 in the Major League Baseball Divisional Series. This was the precarious position that the San Francisco Giants found themselves in against the Cincinnati Reds in October 2012. They had just lost the first two games on their home ground. Morale was at an all-time low, having been trounced 9–0 in the second game and now heading to the lion's den in Cincinnati.

Just before the third game, a fairly new team member decided to take a shot at pepping up his team. Hunter Pence, an outfielder, normally one of the quieter team members, suddenly spoke up to his team in the locker room. He painted the vision again – to win the series. He talked with a burning passion about teamwork, support and how much he desperately wanted to *"play one more day with you guys."* You could hear a pin drop in that locker room.

He had said what was on everyone's mind. They had come so far together, through good days and bad, fighting their way back from losses and injuries over a gruelling season, and now they were on the verge of elimination. Their teammate had pushed the right buttons with his words. The team was fired up, they had found a common, shared purpose and renewed sense of energy and optimism. It was 'rallying time' for the Giants. And then they agreed on their plan to execute.

You can guess what happened next. The Giants went on to win the next three games and eventually came out victorious in the 2012 World Series. Hunter Pence was given a new name by his teammates, and was affectionately called 'The Reverend.' The leader without a title literally changed the game.

I cannot emphasize enough how important it is to be an optimist as a leader. The leader who holds firm in the belief that the team is on the right track, even when things seem to be falling apart and crumbling. We've all experienced moments of self-doubt as leaders. It's especially daunting and stressful when you're faced with grabbing hold of the wheel and steering a ship through rocky waters. And as the water becomes choppier and the storm gets heavier, the game-changing leader knows that this is the moment to dig in. Because it's not in the good times that the team looks to the leader for support, encouragement and leadership. It's during the tough times that all eyes are on the leader.

Clearly, when I look at all of the exceptional leaders I've met over the years, they share at least one common trait. They are, by nature, optimistic. They bring positivity wherever they go. They don't pour sugar on the story. And when times are tough or things are not moving at the expected pace or in the intended direction, they may get frustrated, but they turn that frustration into positive energy and action for change.

Take the Dalai Lama, for instance. For more than five decades, he has tirelessly campaigned for nonviolence of thought and action and for democracy. He has travelled across nations, meeting leaders and religious heads with an immense optimism to achieve his vision of a world of peace. In a world divided, he promotes the bold notion of interreligious harmony.

GAME-CHANGING LEADERS EMBRACE THE BIGGEST CHALLENGES.

AND THEY SHINE MOST WHEN THE STORM ARRIVES.

And he has followers, lots of them. The Dalai Lama has a compelling vision, which he shares with the world. And he works hard with others to influence change. With nearly nine million followers on Twitter alone, he has created a movement. Game-changing leaders radiate positive energy and, even while others doubt them, they stay the course.

As we work through the 'storming' stage of **execute**, each team member and each team collectively will gradually develop new skills and capabilities. As leaders, we need to allow this to happen. Through hands-on experience, they are learning to adapt, to overcome barriers, to fall down, get back up, pivot and move forward again.

I am not a big fan of the 'slow and steady wins the race' philosophy. I prefer my teams to be fuelled by a sense of urgency, supported by a commitment to stay the course. The game-changing leader doesn't have to create a burning platform, though. Instead, focus your message and your energy on creating a burning ambition.

So, here's the dilemma we often face as leaders on a mission to change the game. Several weeks (or months) ago, you carefully crafted your bold and compelling vision. During those long walks in the park or the bottomless cups of coffee at the neighbourhood café, you drafted it, refined it, polished it and, just to be safe, polished it one more time. Then, one fine day with the support of your marketing team, you set out on your omnichannel strategy to express the vision to everyone who would listen. You touched your team from all angles, relentless in your mission to generate excitement and inspire them to get up, to take action. The good news is that your message started to touch a nerve, people were leaning in, you had laid the seeds of a movement. Next, you worked with your support team to gather the tools needed to bring the vision to life. You promised your team that you would provide the tools they needed, and you delivered. And then you stood back and said, "Go for it."

Three days later, three weeks later, three months later … little or no progress. This is another moment of truth. As we learned earlier, in times of challenge and adversity, our reflexive management skills are activated. Let's take a look at how your reflex impacts the **execute** phase.

BUILD **YOUR REFLEX**

Each one of us has a default reaction to the situations we face. Both in times of happiness or frustration, we respond naturally and instinctively. When it comes to the **execute** phase, it's important for you as the leader to adjust your reflexive management style through each step of the process. As you move from **enable** to **execute**, you need to become a facilitator. Which means, you provide opportunities for your team to take on more responsibilities, to work autonomously, to make their own decisions, to learn from failing and to move on. Yet, you need to be around to provide support when they need it. To advise them when they hit blind spots. The leader needs to do all of this from the front, middle and back. It's therefore critical that they play different roles throughout the **execute** process.

Your reflexes may say it's time to grab the wheel and *lead from the front*. When, in fact, that may be the moment when you need to move to the role as *leader from the side*, prompting the team to find the answer themselves, to ignite the engine on their own. Or perhaps you need to shift to the *leader from behind*, supporting and cheering the team on, not telling, not guiding, simply giving words of encouragement as they work their way through the maze of **execute**. In allowing the team to develop and enhance their skills, the leader creates a team that gains confidence, agility and self-reliance. And yes, your job becomes much easier when this happens, allowing you to focus on your rocks.

A word of caution here. Most teams start out on track, heading toward their North Star as defined by the leader and energized by their strong sense of belief. They'll start off with a lot of excitement, inspiration and energy. But the sprint can slow down to a jog and, over time, to a leisurely stroll, if the leader fails to repeat the message. Remember, it was the greater purpose and your compelling vision that brought the team this far in the first place. One of your rocks, then, is to continue to fuel their fire.

This is particularly true in an environment of abundant options, opportunities and choices to move in different directions. So the leader needs to always move forward, providing the team the assurance of support even as they challenge their people. This is a delicate balance of pushing and pulling and of motivating high fives and critical candour. Of being a confidante and the voice of reason that admonishes when required.

Throughout the journey of **execute**, there are many ways to light the spark and fuel the fire in your team. By giving credit where it's due. By celebrating milestones along the way. By recognizing and rewarding people for excellence. By enhancing their presence and making them a high-profile team as they move forward.

And handling surprises, too. There is no getting away from surprises in the voyage of execute. They can come in the form of unpredictable outcomes that we did not have on our road map. Or as offshoots of our efforts. Some of them could be pleasant and positive, others not so. And some of them could well be serendipitous, and amazing discoveries and opportunities, which can lead us to the next vision and mission.

Use the **execute** phase as a learning opportunity. Make sure that the learning is recognized, discussed and put into action. Because what we do know is that learning organizations are stronger and higher performing. This has been proven time and time again.

The naval aviation wing of most naval forces in the world is a great example of a true learning organization – and of execution excellence. Their high performance comes from their learning, and much of their learning comes from the meticulous way they debrief everything – every endeavour, every training, every achievement, every mistake. Trivial or great, basic or complex, small or big, routine or impactful – every action lends itself to a deep learning process. The cycle of prep, team briefing, implementation and debrief is really the essence of successful execution. Help your teams make this an integral part of their operational process, so that their daily tasks become interesting learning opportunities.

It's at this point that we come full circle on execution. This is where game-changing action happens. Everything else has been setting the stage for this moment, where the pieces make the picture. However well you may think you have accomplished the four phases of **envision**, **express**, **excite** and **enable**, **execute** still remains the ultimate judge of your efforts.

Leaders on a mission to make an impact must be careful not to fall prey to what I call the 'hollow egg syndrome' – to become someone who tells a good story, looks good on the surface but lacks substance and is unable to deliver.

Let's push pause for a moment to summarize what we've learned.
- Execute is a journey; it happens in stages.
- Execute requires both processes and 'common sense.'
- Execute is directly connected to the engagement of the leader. Be engaged enough to facilitate and empower your team to move with freedom, achieve success and grow in the process.
- Execute gains momentum with small steps forward. Celebrate the successes.
- Execute breeds followership. Share the spotlight with the team.

Now, let's take a look at the process that follows and think about the phenomenon called 'breakthrough.' How does it typically work in an organization? We have the launch where we create the base. We then create the momentum. Momentum leads us to a very important moment that may or may not materialize. If it does, we call it the breakthrough. A competent manager typically ends up in the momentum zone. He runs a tight ship and efficiently maintains the status quo. There is nothing wrong with this – but it's not path-breaking leadership.

Breakthrough comes when we move beyond being a competent leader and beyond maintaining the status quo. It happens when we challenge our assumptions and start taking risks outside our comfort zones. It calls on us to do things we have never done before and bring our teams along on the journey, encouraging them to do the same. Breakthrough ideas come in all shapes and sizes – and at different times, too. While there isn't a single pattern, there are some ways to ignite and accelerate at the execution stage.

TIPS: EXECUTE TO 'MAKE IT HAPPEN'

Execute begins at the envision stage.
A compelling vision is the key driver of flawless execution. Revisit your vision to make sure it's bold, ambitious and strongly rooted in purpose.

And how about we think of execute as embedded into every other E – something that streams through each one of them?
Right from the time you meet with and actively listen to your people to **envision** to the time you plan the **express** activity to **excite** your teams and **enable** them with tools and support systems, **execute** courses through your every action. Everything you do sets the stage to **execute**.

**Game-changing leadership is the sum of the five Es,
but it's also a multiple of them all.**
Your effectiveness as a leader depends on how you ignite the
multiplier effect. If one of the Es is ignored or not given the
focus and attention it deserves, your impact weakens.

It's therefore up to you as the leader on a mission to change
the game to ensure that the Es are strong for an impeccable
execute finale. Ensure your discerning eye picks up the people
who go the extra mile, giving 150% to the effort, versus those
who are half-hearted. Celebrating and recognizing those who
are committed to bringing the vision to life sends out a clear
message. For the others, it's time for courageous conversations.
High-performing teams live by the '100% rule': give it everything
you've got, every single time. When it comes to **execute**, the
devil does indeed lie in the small details.

Beware of when novelty turns into routine.
Innovation, sometimes, can be the enemy of consistent excellence.
We quickly get excited by the newness of ideas and actions
simply because they tend to push our motivational buttons to
excel at something different.

You need to kick-start a new mini-cycle of **'envision–express–
excite–enable'** when your team masters the new routine and
it becomes a templatized one. Otherwise, sloppiness can creep
silently into **execute**. Your responsibility is to keep the motivation
of mastery intact of doing something the 101st time with the
same fervour as they would do the first time.

"WELL DONE IS BETTER THAN WELL SAID."

BENJAMIN FRANKLIN

Transparency of individual, team and organization performance can be a way to sustain execution excellence. Add a smattering of creative gamification, and you may just brew the perfect concoction for a culture that inspires high performance. A culture that pushes your people to excel for its sake and not for anything else.

And then, of course, the vital ingredient – discipline.
Discipline is the key to bridging knowledge with action. It can be incorporated in many ways, such as through pulse checks and compass meetings, or great conversations and engaging regularly with your senior leaders, managers and employees, in groups and in one-on-one discussions. By tracking progress against plans with relevant metrics, timely course corrections can be made. A culture of discipline leads to a healthy cadence, which, in turn, creates momentum.

GOLDEN NUGGETS
EXECUTE

Execute is the measurable moment of truth.

Look around for the giants and then stand on their shoulders.

People drive technology and processes. If technology and processes are key parts of your execution, make sure you have the right people.

Be prepared to fall down, get back up and move forward. Successful execution comes on the back of trips and falls. Winning teams always bounce back.

When the action begins, sometimes 'good' is good enough. But to accelerate into the day after tomorrow, be relentless in leading the team to great.

Focus on the rocks, the tools and actions that will trigger acceleration. Push the pebbles aside; they will take care of themselves.

Leading outstanding execution requires consistency, grit, passion and optimism. Start each day with optimism and the rest will fall into place.

CHAPTER 8

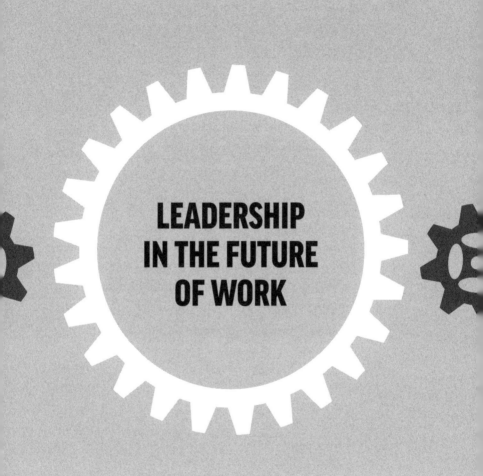

LEADERSHIP
IN THE FUTURE
OF WORK

L eaders have a lot of attributes in common, whether in business, sports, government, non-profit organizations, or family and society. One common denominator is that we share the responsibility to take the people around us 'forward,' to lead them into the future.

Ask the people you work with a simple question: "When you hear the word 'future,' what does it mean to you?" I expect you'll discover that most people will talk about tomorrow, or perhaps three, five or ten years hence. Or maybe 50–100 years later, in the case of the big dreamers.

At our current rate of change, being prepared for tomorrow is simply not good enough. We need to stay ahead of the change curve, constantly preparing for the day after tomorrow. Future-proof leaders need to read the signals from the world around them and leverage a combination of technology, data and gut instinct to make decisions. And, most important, they should never stop experimenting.

In 1965, Gordon Moore, the cofounder of INTEL, claimed that we can expect the speed and capability of our computers to increase every couple of years, even as we will pay less for them. The same applies to leadership. Leaders need to evolve and reinvent themselves frequently. Maybe every two years is a stretch – but certainly, game-changing leaders are always eager to learn and stay ahead of the curve. They do this by investing time, effort and resources in their personal growth and development. It's no wonder that leadership coaching as an industry has gained traction. The significant increase in the number of executive

MBA programs around the world is evidence of leaders eager to sharpen their swords to make an impact.

An exciting stage is unfolding before us. Some things we already know:

- **A future of work that is fluid.**
  New jobs are being created faster than we can imagine. It was only three years ago when most of us had no idea what a data scientist or AI analyst was!

- **New dimensions of diversity in the workforce.**
  Millennials, Gen Zs and the Generation Alphas, the children of today's oldest millennials (described as 'Millennials on steroids'), have redefined diversity. The workforce of the future is set in a different mold and will require different styles of leadership.

- **A redefined and rewritten concept of freedom of work location and content.**
  A world where the concept of 'work-life balance' becomes 'work-life integration.'

- **A workplace where mindfulness becomes 'mindfull'-ness.**
  Especially with the democratization of information.

- **A workforce where technology helps us connect for touch.**
  At the same time, and in spite of the fast-swirling changes, – there is one timeless constant. That is effective leadership. This is the kind of leadership that is personal, a reflection of your unique strengths, passion and beliefs. It's what you will apply in the adventure ahead of you with the elements of the E5 that you will personalize with your own touch.

THE PAST IS WHERE YOU LEARNED THE LESSON.

THE FUTURE IS WHERE YOU *APPLY* THE LESSON.

Many of us started our careers before the computer was common in the workplace. Today's Millennials are the generation of radical change. They grew up in a world of technology first, both in the way they work and how they communicate. The speed of change they've encountered is astounding. This generation embraces it; they literally live on the cutting edge and are constantly searching for new, 'better ways' to get things done. At the same time, they value purpose and are urged to be mindful. But how can someone be mindful, fully in the moment and engaged in their world of constant disruption and interruption? It's no wonder they chat using mysterious acronyms and in short bits and bytes.

As Millennials continue to rise in the workforce, there are at least three generations ahead of them on the journey, products of a very different way of working and communicating. These are the generations that were taught to think broadly, to express themselves, to expand on their ideas. And somehow these very different animals need to get along.

There is a clear sense of alienation on both sides of the room. The Millennials gathered on one side of the room, at standing desks, on beanbag chairs, munching on snacks as they trade ideas back and forth.

Millennials may see some Baby Boomers as obsolete, and some Baby Boomers feel phased out. The Gen-Z may feel frustrated, even shackled by slower and outdated practices. Hence, the phrase, "Okay, Boomer," was born. And Gen-Xers may feel lost as part of a sandwich demographic. Leaders need to connect across generations, understanding what makes each group tick, finding their motivational buttons and pushing them in a way that unites.

As leaders, we need to be 'futurists.' I did not coin this word, I assure you – there are actually job titles to this effect. As a futurist, you will need to recognize trends, evaluate their impact, and strategize to build a vision around them, express it, inspire to action and implement for success. Sound familiar? You could say that the E5 was born out of my quest to build future-proofed teams.

Arthur C Clarke, author of *2001: A Space Odyssey*, shared his futurist take on the world. Coincidentally, also in 1964, in an interview with the BBC, he specifically talked about the future of work and the workplace. He envisioned video calls being commonplace in the future. He described a workplace that was not limited to being physically present in the same location – and called it telecommuting. He also conjured a vision of a network that could enable us to send information, to exchange pictorial information, data and even books. He was labelled nuts – until the internet and email conquered the scene.

Do you see a pattern here? Visionaries preparing for the day after tomorrow, not only predicting but *creating* the future of work. Creating your vision of the future is one thing but making a conscious choice to pursue it is another. This decision-making process is a very important aspect of leadership. We all face forks in our journey and, for many leaders, difficult choices arise on a daily basis. Some of these decisions affect people and are deeply rooted in emotions, while others are about the metrics and are data-driven. The impactful leader mixes logic and emotion in making decisions. This is especially valuable for leaders in the early stage of their journey. Establish good habits in decision-making. Have a robust decision-making filter. This will serve all leaders well on the path ahead.

There is a saying made famous by motivational speaker Jim Rohn: "We are the average of the five people we spend the most time with." I would take it one step further. Strong leaders make a clear decision to surround themselves with game changers, with fellow leaders on a mission to make an impact. We raise our game when we surround ourselves with leaders who are passionate about everything they do – starting with creating a compelling vision and building followership, a movement to action and ultimately seeing the vision come to life. As leaders, we are the average of the leaders we surround ourselves with. So it's important to choose wisely and carefully.

Seasoned leaders realize that they need advice from time to time – so they surround themselves with people who support, challenge and give the good advice they seek. Perhaps this is the one commitment that I've made as a leader – and this has helped me grow and thrive over the years. Impactful leaders constantly strive to learn from their own experiences and from those of others. They build relationships with other leaders, those who have made bold moves to step out of their own comfort zones and who are ready to share their discoveries with fellow seekers.

I'm a big believer in learning from the past. I have seen and led organizations struggling to survive in difficult situations, with weak spirit, culture and values. My 22 years in Japan also taught me a few things about how to deal with challenges – the first is that every problem has a solution. In Japan that means embracing *kaizen* – meticulous analysis, identifying bottlenecks, and committing to relentless focus on execution when approaching a problem.

I bring these valuable lessons I learned in Japan with me wherever I go. "Every problem has a solution" has served me well across borders. In charting your own course for the future, find your purpose and your guiding principles. Look to the past and honour it as you focus on the future.

Anyone who has earned an MBA over the past 15 years or attended executive education courses has at some time encountered the Kodak and Fujifilm story. It's a poignant tale of two companies, competing toe-to-toe in the camera, film and development business. When the emergence of digital quickly arrived around 2000, Kodak chose to hold firm on their strategy to win market share in the camera, film and processing segments. In 2001, revenues were at an all-time high and the board of Kodak approved a 'full speed ahead' mantra to win more market share from its rival Fujifilm.

Meanwhile the CEO of Fujifilm, Shigetaka Komori, quickly recognized the danger in this strategy. As he said, "A peak always conceals a treacherous valley." He saw the storm brewing well before it arrived: that film cameras, film and processing/developing would one day become obsolete. Fujifilm chose a different path, one that gradually pivoted away from its core business, the heritage and foundation on which the company was built, and embraced the digital movement and the revolutionary changes to the photography industry that followed.

Komori devised a plan that he would later say was focused on saving the company from disaster. This vision was crafted under the guise of the upcoming 75th anniversary of the group when in fact it was about survival. Komori and his leadership team laid the foundation for a diversified portfolio, leveraging their strong capabilities and patents, and expansion into the diagnostic imaging segment. In spite of the clear shift in consumer behaviour, Kodak held firm to their strategy. They fell into the trap of playing catch-up and in 2006, their CEO was quoted as saying, "Digital cameras is a crappy business." The rest, of course, is history.

Let's turn our attention to the workplace of the future – liquid, borderless and digital. Omnichannel experiences will rule for all stakeholders. Work will be a blend of virtual and face-to-face interactions, both for the individual and teams. Cisco's connected workspaces and GE's FastWorks approach have hit the sweet spot in bringing lean start-up practices that empower employees to make speedy and unfettered decisions regarding their work and learning.

Get ready for the liquefaction of the workforce as the new normal, with a blend of full-time, contingent and gig workers. Can you be agile in your leadership to provide your workforce the freedom to choose their project and even their boss?

Sure, technology will play an important role in the future of work. In the age of man and machine, how will you look at collaboration, trust, creative thinking and mentorship? They will still be critical core skills, only they have to be done differently. That is why I call it 'tech for touch.'

In order to lead your team into the day after tomorrow, it's crucial to be relentless in communicating your vision. Communicate in a storytelling and 'anecdatal' (a term I coined, using stories with an element of data weaved in together to communicate a compelling message) way. Communicate to connect. Be an advocate of your team and their shared mission to bring your vision to life; support and mentor them. And communicate your intentions to do so with authenticity and clarity.

This is the story of a leader who, nearly 40 years ago, dared to look at the future of work with vision, foresight – and extreme courage. The year was 1971. Darwin Smith took over as CEO of Kimberly-Clark. The company's core business was the production of coated paper. For years, it had enjoyed unprecedented leadership. True, margins were eroding, but there was really no competition in sight.

Smith trained his sights on the day after tomorrow, even as tomorrow was looking relatively comfortable. He came to the decision that coated paper as a business would certainly decline. Consumer paper products was the place to be, he envisioned. But here was the catch. Although on an upswing, consumer paper products was a highly competitive and crowded area. And the company would have to take on giants such as

Procter & Gamble. Shoot for the greater greatness? Or suffer the slow perish? Smith opted for the former. And so, Kimberly-Clark sold their mills and re-invested it all in the consumer business. Brands like Huggies and Kleenex were thus born.

And here is the answer to leaders who may ask the question: "What if I am not charismatic? How can I pull off my vision to inspire my people?" Smith was such a leader – and he showed how. He offered no grandiose vision statement or a hyped change program. He inspired his people with authentic questions. What could Kimberly-Clark be passionate about? What could it be best at? With what could it rule the markets and multiply its economics?

For months he continued to ask these questions in an unassuming but earnest manner, but with tremendous conviction. He expressed it with more than enough inspiration to excite his team. And he enabled them amid considerable derision from Wall Street analysts, pundits and the media.

It was a turnaround that was as stunning as it was outstanding. Kimberly-Clark became the leading company in the consumer paper industry – beating Procter & Gamble in six of eight product categories and acquiring its main competitor, Scott Paper. Not only this, but it went on to easily outperform biggies such as Hewlett-Packard, General Electric and Coca-Cola by clear miles.

From a struggling industrial giant to the leader in paper-based consumer products company in the world – what do you think made it possible? It was Smith's ability to think beyond tomorrow to the day after and lead people to see how their work was for the greater good of the organization and its people.

Recall in the chapter on express, we learned about Mike Babcock, one of the winningest coaches in ice hockey history. At the time of the writing of this book, Babcock had just been fired by the Toronto Maple Leafs. He had left a winning program as coach of the Detroit Red Wings on a mission to transform the Maple Leafs, a storied organization with a long history, but a hockey team that was in disarray. For Babcock, his vision was to achieve key milestones on the way to achieving his bold vision – ultimately, to take a losing team and transform them into winning the coveted Stanley Cup, from the bottom to becoming champions. To be fair, during his five seasons as the coach of the Maple Leafs, he led the team from last place in the league to qualifying for the play-offs, an exceptional accomplishment. He also made tough decisions along the way, injecting new energy and fresh, young talent into the team. However, while the team made the play-offs in each season under his tenure, they failed to make it past the first round. In order to win the Stanley Cup the team needs to win four rounds of series based on winning four games out of seven. Within the context of the E5, Babcock had crafted a bold vision, and while he wasn't a media favourite, he did a good job of expressing his vision to the public but, more importantly, to his players. When he first arrived in Toronto, the veterans and new players alike were excited by the conviction of this legendary coach. They believed they could do it. He further enabled the team to win by strengthening each position, making trades to other teams in exchange for higher-skilled players. However, Babcock was unable to build a solid defensive core, which ultimately proved to be the key barrier to winning games against the strong offensive teams. And while he worked hard with his coaches and the veteran players to execute on his strategy, he simply was unable to build the strong sense of followership from the younger players. And over time, the faith in their coach started to waver. He started to leave doubt, which ultimately led to his removal from the organization. There is debate on whether his coaching style was too rooted in the old school. Some doubters claim that while he may have had success in the past with his approach, this latest outcome is a sign that Babcock has been unable to reinvent himself, a key quality of a game-changing leader.

Marshall Goldsmith, in his book *What Got You Here, Won't Get You There*,[24] eloquently points out that effective leaders focus on behaviours, the soft skills, not on their technical expertise or the hard skills they possess. And many of the traits and behaviours that have brought you from there to here may not be the vehicle to take you into the future. We must constantly innovate and experiment, learn, fail, apologize, try again and grow stronger. And each step of the way, staying humble and appreciative of the opportunity to participate in the journey.

In retrospect, Babcock's impact began to weaken at the enable stage, which led to an inability to execute on bringing his bold vision to life with a new group of players. We can debate on whether the legendary coach failed on his mission – clearly he achieved some remarkable milestones that were triggers to bring the team closer to their BHAG. But he wasn't able to win the cup in Toronto, the key measurable outcome of the success of his vision. With a long track record of creating winning teams, you can bet that Babcock will bounce back with another team on a renewed mission to lead the players and the fans toward bringing his next bold vision to life. And it will happen when he 'honours the past and focuses on the future.'

Game-changing leaders are visionaries. That's not to say they are fortune tellers. In fact, the futurists I've met tell me that they anticipate the future by looking closely at the trends of the past. They look for cycles and universal truths. So, you could say that visionary leaders are futurists, always on the search for revealing trends. Sometimes this requires 'in-the-box' thinking, revisiting things we already know.

For example, Maslow said that humans have five basic needs – physiological, safety, love and belonging, esteem and self-actu-alization. Perhaps there is another – the desire to be inspired and led. Gandhi, Mother Teresa and the Dalai Lama, all exceptional leaders in their own right, also had a unique ability to inspire to action and to create a sense of followership. They did this by crafting and sharing a compelling vision (envision). We can be sure they made time to think and reflect. They went back to what we already know, lesson learned over generations and eras gone by, that some things are both borderless and timeless. And in the process, they became visionary leaders.

Imagine the potent combination of a vision that touches the minds and hearts of people – and crystal-clear communication (express) that truly connects with them. It creates the stage for the next level of the hierarchical pyramid – the freedom of passion (excite). The leader with purpose has an extraordinary opportunity to lead people to do well, and do *good*. To excel individually, as a team and to make a positive impact on the world in the process. Here is where you play the role of an igniter, exciting your people with a picture of a future of opportunities. You transform work to a *purpose* that fuels your people.

Go ahead, create your own recipe of leadership. Like a wise person once said: "Whether you can or cannot, you are right."

CHAPTER 9

NOW IT'S
YOUR TURN

The E5 has been my trusty companion as I navigated the choppy seas of leadership. And that's what makes it special – it's a framework that is useful for anyone who is on a quest to craft their own personalized brand of leadership.

ENVISION, EXPRESS, EXCITE, ENABLE, EXECUTE. NOW IT'S *YOUR* TURN.

Leaders don't have a crystal ball. Neither do we wake up one morning with all of our questions about the future answered. The **envision** wheel helps you start the right way, and when things get foggy, it keeps you focused and on course. It's a compass that enables you to create a strong vision that is compelling, focused on tomorrow and tugs at the heartstrings of the people – with purpose and cause. Regardless of the weather, these things never change.

Express challenges you to come up with a way to share the vision with your teams with a power-packed punch. In a way that's crystal clear, connects and is easy to understand. And it taps into our collective energy, encouraging the team to lean in for more.

Having created a buzz, look to **excite** to ignite the new interest to action. To feed the sense of excitement, which then becomes contagious – this is so crucial to success in bringing the vision to life. Excite is your chance to be an authentic voice, to share your passion and use this to influence the team to ask the question, "When can we start?!"

And then comes the important turning point, where you can say, *my vision* becomes *our vision*; the team is eager to go but they need the tools to bring the vision to life. It's your chance to **enable**, to ensure the team has the skills, knowledge and resources required to move the wheel, in the process creating a sense of confidence on your team. It's at this stage that the team begins to believe that *we can do it.*

The moment of truth has arrived. All of the hard work done in the stages of **envision**, **express**, **excite** and **enable** come together now to set the stage to **execute**. One step closer to changing the game.

You can move freely to any of the five gears based on your needs, and the needs of your team at that moment. This freedom that the leader enjoys can also be the biggest challenge: knowing which E to focus on and when to do so. Remember, every leadership challenge is unique, just like every leader. You have your distinct strengths that you must leverage in placing your signature on your own leadership. You can navigate between the five Es in a manner that meets your specific needs. And you can introduce a few more Es or, if you prefer, make it As, Bs or Cs. Because it's not about *my* five Es. It's about creating your own formula to becoming a game-changing leader. Your leadership should be authentic. It should reflect your experiences, rooted in who you are and what you stand for, your own greater purpose. It should be entirely *you*.

On the E5 journey, we've learned that leadership is both an art and science. The outstanding leaders who have walked before us found a way to blend both elements for impact. We should learn from them. In some way, we're the product of both the best and worst leaders we've worked with and observed over the years. And we learn valuable lessons from both. We borrow some qualities from the best leaders and vehemently reject some of the traits and behaviours of the worst. And in the process, our own personal version of leadership is born.

There is a quote often attributed to Winston Churchill, although some say it was said by George Tilton. It's often used by coaches of professional sports teams and CEOs. Regardless of where it came from, it's a powerful message for any leader on a mission to make a dent in the universe: "Success is not final, failure is not fatal: it is the courage to continue that counts."

Now the stage is yours. It's your turn to forge your personal stamp of leadership. And, in the process of crafting your version of leadership, you'll also come up with your own '*ism*,' your unique formula to change the game. And I'm sure it will serve you well.

Here's wishing you the best on your own E5 journey … Let's change the game together.

GOLDEN NUGGETS
LEADERSHIP

Outstanding leaders seek challenges. They embrace adversity and ambiguity. They step out of their comfort zone every chance they get.

Game-changing leaders are influencers. They influence their teams not to play the game better, but instead to create the game.

Leadership is defined by behaviour. Exceptional leadership then, requires exceptional behaviour.

A compelling vision is not so much about the 'what' as it's about the 'why.' A solid vision, with a strongly rooted purpose, sets the team up for success.

Craft a bold vision that pushes the motivational buttons for every member of the team.

Communicate your vision in a way that matters. Make it real for your people. Use an omnichannel strategy to ignite the fire that encourages them to believe.

Listen to your team, grasp their language.
Then communicate your vision in their language.

Excite your team with the 'why.' Paint the picture of the journey.
Give them the opportunity to be part of something special.

Excitement comes from being connected. To be a
game-changing leader, be present. Be in the game.

Enabling leaders commit to providing the environment,
skills and tools for the team to succeed.

Technology and processes don't change the game.
People do. Enable your people to be game changers.

Use the execute phase to learn. Push pause,
celebrate milestones and confront the setbacks.
Fall down, learn, move forward.

As a leader be a futurist. Lead your team
into the day after tomorrow.

Craft your own version of the E5.
Take it to the world and change the game.

Stay focused on your North Star.

Be relentless to bring your vision to reality.

REFERENCES

1. Dan Cable, *Alive at Work: The neuroscience of helping your people love what they do*, Harvard Business Review Press, 2018.

2. Jim Collins, *Good to Great: Why some companies make the leap ... and others don't*, Harper Business, 2001.

3. Per-Ola Karlsson, Martha Turner and Peter Gassmann, "Succeeding the long-serving legend in the corner office," *Strategy&*, 2019, strategy-business.com/article/Succeeding-the-long-serving-legend-in-the-corner-office?gko=90171.

4. Dan Roam, *The Back of the Napkin*, Portfolio Hardcover, 2008.

5. Hope Solo, "Players tell themselves the World Cup final is just another game. They're wrong," The Guardian, July 6, 2019, https://www.theguardian.com/football/2019/jul/06/players-tell-themselves-the-world-cup-final-is-just-another-game-theyre-wrong.

6. Robin Sharma, *The 5 AM Club: Own your morning, elevate your life*, HaperCollins, 2018.

7. Mats Alvesson, Martin Blom and Stefan Sveningsson, *Reflexive Leadership: Organizing in an imperfect world*, Sage Publications, 2017.

8. Steve Jobs' iPod launch address, October 23, 2001.

9. Salim Ismail, Yuri van Geest, Michael S Malone and Peter H Diamandis, *Exponential Organizations: Why new organizations are ten times better, faster and cheaper than yours (and what to do about it)*, Diversion Books, 2014.

10. "The 2018 Amazon Shopper Behavior Study," CPC strategy, last accessed April 7, 2020, http://learn.cpcstrategy.com/ rs/006-GWW-889/images/2018-Amazon-Shopper-Behavior-Study.pdf.

11. Mike Babcock and Rick Larsen, *Leave No Doubt: A credo for chasing your dreams*, McGill-Queen's University Press, 2012.

12. Coach Herb Brooks' address to the US Olympic hockey team before the USSR match, 1980, Lake Placid, New York.

13. Mary Bellis, "Thomas Edison's 'Muckers,'" *ThoughtCo.*, updated January 28, 2019, https://www.thoughtco.com/ thomas-edisons-muckers-4071190.

14. "Historic Documents: The Gettysburg Address," US history, last accessed April 7, 2020, ushistory.org/documents/gettysburg.htm.

15. John Dragoon, "Ted Sorensen's Gift to Marketing," *Forbes*, April 12, 2011, https://www. forbes.com/sites/johndragoon/2011/04/12/ ted-sorensens-gift-to-marketing/#1340213248ce.

16. Douglas A Ready, "Getting Employees Excited About a New Direction," *Harvard Business Review*, November 20, 2015, https://hbr.org/2015/11/ getting-employees-excited-about-a-new-direction.

17. Samantha Liddle, "From Liverpool to the Toppermost of the Poppermost," Angel Fire, last accessed April 7, 2020, http:// www.angelfire.com/pa2/stella/fanfic.html.

18. Rik Vera, *Managers the Day After Tomorrow*, Lannoo Publishers, 2019.

19. "Home page," 30% Club, last accessed April 7, 2020, https://30percentclub.org.

20. For more details, read: Boris Groysberg et. al., "Womenomics in Japan," *Harvard Business School*, February 1, 2017.

21. "Standing on the shoulders of giants," Wikipedia, last accessed April 7, 2020, https://en.wikipedia.org/wiki/Standing_on_the_shoulders_of_giants.

22. "DiSC Overview," Discprofile, last accessed April 7, 2020, https://www.discprofile.com/what-is-disc/overview/.

23. Angela Duckworth, *Grit: The power of passion and perseverance*, Collins, 2016.

24. Marshall Goldsmith, *What Got You Here Won't Get You There: How successful people become even more successful*, Hyerion, 2007.

BIBLIOGRAPHY/ FURTHER READING

Jim Collins, *Good to Great*, Harper Business, 2001.

W Chan Kim and Renée Mauborgne, *Blue Ocean Strategy*, Harvard Business Review Press, 2004.

Marshall Goldsmith, *What Got You Here Won't Get You There*, Hyperion, 2007.

Howard Schultz, *Pour Your Heart Into It*, Hachette Books, 1997.

Ken Honda, *Happy Money*, Gallery Books, 2019.

Robin Sharma, *The 5 AM Club*, HarperCollins, 2018.

Dan Cable, *Alive at Work*, Harvard Business Review, 2018.

Mike Babcock and Rick Larsen, *Leave No Doubt*, McGill-Queen's University Press, 2012.

Kenneth Blanchard and Spencer Johnson, *The One Minute Manager*, William Morrow & Company, 2003.

Michael Watkins, *The First 90 Days*, Harvard Business Review, 2013.

Liz Wiseman and Greg McKeown, *Multipliers*, HarperBusiness, 2010.

Brian Tracy, *Speak to Win*, AMACOM, 2008.

Daniel Pink, *Drive*, Riverhead Books, 2009.

Simon Sinek, *Start with Why*, Portfolio, 2009.

Albert Liebermann and Hector Garcia, *Ikigai*, Random House, 2016.

Navi Radjou, Simone Ahuja and Jaideep Prabhu, *Jugaad Innovation: A frugal and flexible approach to innovation for the 21st Century*, Random House, 2012.

David H Maister, *Practise What You Preach*, Free Press, 2001.

Dan Roam, *The Back of the Napkin*, Portfolio Hardcover, 2008.

Salim Ismail, Yuri van Geest, Michael S Malone and Peter H Diamandis, *Exponential Organizations*, Diversion Books, 2014.

Rik Vera, *Managers the Day After Tomorrow*, Lannoo Campus, 2018.

Angela Duckworth, *Grit: The power of passion and perseverance*, Collins, 2016.

Rob Goffee and Gareth Jones, *Why Should Anyone Be Led by You?*, Harvard Business Review Press, 2006.